# GUNFITTING
## The Quest for Perfection

# GUNFITTING

## The Quest for Perfection

## MICHAEL YARDLEY

### Foreword by
## PAUL ROBERTS

• THE •
SPORTSMAN'S
PRESS
*LONDON*

Published by The Sportsman's Press 1993
Reprinted 1996
Reprinted 1999
© Michael Yardley 1993

Line illustrations by Clive Rawden and the author

A catalogue record for this book
is available from the British Library

ISBN 0-948253-65-7

Photoset and printed in Great Britain by
Redwood Books Limited, Trowbridge, Wiltshire

# CONTENTS

# ACKNOWLEDGEMENTS

To complete this project I have sought advice and information from many different sources; now is my chance to say thank you to all those people who have given so generously of their time and knowledge. My old friend Alan Rose, Chief Instructor at the West London Shooting Grounds has shared his great knowledge with me over many years, and gave me the base upon which I built my own understanding of this subject. There are other very talented and experienced individuals whose help has been crucial – Andrew Perkins, Senior Instructor at Holland & Holland; Richard Ford, Chief Instructor at the Parkford Shooting Centre; Graeme Rimer, Keeper of Firearms at the Royal Armouries at the Tower of London; Alan Rhone of Vari-comb fame, and gunsmith Mark Crudgington, of I.M. Crudgington of Bath. Jan Stevenson, editor of *Handgunner* magazine, also deserves a very special place in my roll of honour; he has helped this project in inumerable ways. He provided office space at a time of crisis; he has always made himself available when I have been in need of someone with whom to talk through a technical point; he has acted as thesaurus, encylopaedia and dictionary, not to mention proof reader – and all with good humour and infinite patience.

I would also like to acknowledge the generous help given by: Kenneth Kemp, Sue Coley, Clive and Diana Rawden, Garry Coward-Williams, Ray Hulston, Ian Cawthorne, Maggie Lacchin, Malcolm Mackender, Judith White, Alexandra Foley, Mike Baldwin, Ken Davies, Brian Hebditch, Ed Paine, Christopher Brunker, Jed Stevenson, David Peel, Andrew Young, John Richardson, Alistair Ford, Bob Clarke, Morlin Ellis, Frank Tanzi, John Rosenberg, Paul Roberts, Carl Bloxham, Roland Wild, Trevor Scott, Fiona Yardley, Phillip Jarratt, Richard Law, Elizabeth Law, Malcolm Jenkins, John and Vivien Yardley, Andy Marshall, Bill Rudrum, Piers Crump, Mark Renmant, Frederick Wilkinson, Kevin Gill, Mike George, Mike Barnes, Mark Murrayflutter, John Resteghini, Bob Bonham, Bernard Cole, Gordon Swatton, Mark Elliot, Malcolm Grendon, Mark Course and Robert Frampton.

As well as all those mentioned above I would like to note my indebtedness, to certain authors past and present: W.W.Greener, Harold Peterson, J.H.Walsh, Robert Churchill, Percy Stanbury and Gordon Carlisle, G.T.Teasedale-Buckell, John Brindle, Jack O'Connor, Barney Hartman, Bruce Bowlen, Adam Bogardus, Art Blatt, W.H.B.Smith and Joseph Smith, G.T.Garwood (*aka* Gough Thomas), Gerald Burrard, Charles Chenevix Trench, Chris Cradock, Ian.V.Hogg, Hugh Pollard, H.A.A.Thorn (*aka* Charles Lancaster), Don Zutz, Kay Ohye, Charles Askins, Elmer Keith, Geoffrey Boothroyd, Robert Arthur, Arthur Hearn, Bob Brister, Wayne Martin, and Richard Akehurst.

Whilst acknowledging the direct and indirect input of many individuals into this book it goes without saying that I alone take full responsibility for everything which is presented here.

# LIST OF PLATES

10   A paper pattern plate.
     Master gunfitter Andrew Perkins measures a gun for length to middle.

11   Right and left eye dominance and central vision.
     Making an alteration to a Boss try gun.

12   Paul Roberts, Chairman of John Rigby & Co, measuring drop at comb
     and heel.
     An Italian jig used by Gunmark for measuring over-and-unders.
     Another measuring device, used at the shooting grounds of the London
     gunmakers Boss.

13   A schnabel forend on a Beretta 682 Supersports.
     A plain but elegant and practical forend on a Beretta 686.
     A forend with finger grooves on a Miroku shotgun.
     The beavertail forend on a Beretta side-by-side.

14   The adjustable trigger on a Browning gun.
     The trigger on this Winchester has been subtly modified by a London-
     trained craftsman.
     Disabled shooters present a special challenge to the gunfitter.

15   The Hydro-Coil stock for reducing recoil.
     Craftsman Mark Course checks that the comb on a modified Beretta 682
     is level.
     A German machine sometimes used at Gunmark for bending stocks.

16   The gunfitter strives to create a gun which is a natural extension of arms
     and eyes.

# FOREWORD

For many years I have struggled with a diversity of gun measurements supplied by various gunfitters for people of the same size and in some cases different sets of measurements for the same person. It is therefore with great pleasure and a large amount of relief that I look forward to the publication of Michael Yardley's very well-researched and easy to follow book.

Having, over thirty years and working from my own observation, 'shop fitted' guns to literally thousands of people and altered as many guns to 'measurements supplied' by professional gunfitters, I am absolutely convinced of the importance of correct gun fit.

Michael accurately traces the development of the gun stock shape and the technique of shooting flying which puts into perspective the whole evolution of the fitted shotgun stock as we know it today.

With regard to gunstock shape, we at Rigbys are always torn between the traditional design and the desire to innovate, improve or revert to earlier innovations in gun and rifle stock design. In this respect I have found the book a great source of encouragement to delve deeper into the question of stock shape and gun fit. I think that it will be of immense value to British gun manufacturers who have, in some respects, lagged behind their continental rivals in the forward development of shape and fit of gun stocks. Whilst I appreciate that, at the moment, Britain does not produce mass market shotguns, we are still the guiding influence on the production design of many of the world's top volume gun producers. Firms such as Browning UK, Gunmark (Beretta) and A.S.I. (AYA) have all made huge input into stock designs of their respective imports. To this end Michael Yardley's book will be an invaluable source of information.

I also feel it will be of great help in moving forward the design quality of the stocks being produced by the twenty or so manufacturers of best English shotguns still active in the United Kingdom today.

In his book Michael Yardley rediscovers many gems of information, some long buried, concerning such features as W.W. Greener's note '... [a gun stock] in most cases should be slightly shorter to the left edge of the butt plate than to the right (for a right-handed shooter)'. Whilst collating all known traditional information, Yardley is not without innovative theories of his own. For example, the differentials in cast off between side-by-side and over-and-under guns, both being fitted for the same person.

I consider the book a mine of information for both the shooter, the gunfitter and most definitely the gunmaker.

*Paul Roberts*
*Chairman of John Rigby & Co (Gun Makers) Ltd*
*and former Chairman of the Gun Trade Association*

'How many guns fit the shooters correctly? Very few! There are a ton of shooters receiving bumps and bruises ... shooting high and low, to the right or left; missing targets and becoming discouraged due to the fit of the gun. It must mount with ease and comfort, be in level alignment with the eyes, so that it will stay there throughout the act of shooting.'

*Dr Wayne Martin*

'Never, have the stock of a gun bent or cast off to compensate for faults in gun mounting. These should be corrected, not by deforming the gun, but by improving your style.'

*Robert Churchill*

'I should recall to mind that there is at least one case on record where a man was diagnosed by try-gun fitting as having a left master eye, when in fact the eye in question was made of glass.'

*Gough Thomas (G.T. Garwood)*

'The man who really means to shoot well does so irrespective of any trifling wrong dimension in the weapon he has to use, and the acquisition of the art of shooting enables one to do what the hypercritical gun-fitting faddist would not attempt with even the most favourable conditions'

*W.W. Greener*

'It is quite possible for an experienced trick-shot to make allowances even for holding his gun upside down, but why should any man who shoots for pleasure submit to the discomfort of an ill-fitting gun?'

*Charles Lancaster (H.A. Thorn)*

'Any stock that in its back recoil or kick does not automatically relieve the pressure on the cheek is entirely bad. That is, it does not fit the shooter, and it will sooner or later make him afraid of his gun ... '

*G.T. Teasdale-Buckell*

'I take all this gun fitting business with a grain of salt ... I am convinced that there is only one person in the world who can tell a shooter if a shotgun stock fits him or not – and that is the shooter himself, but only if he has done enough shooting to know how a gun should handle, mount and point.'

*Jack O'Connor*

'Be careful in the selection of your first gun, for you will 'grow' to it, and it will always influence you thereafter, perhaps in the wrong way.'

*Charles Askins*

# INTRODUCTION

Gunfit – which in this book is shorthand for the fitting of shotgun to shooter – is a fascinating subject; it is also one upon which there is a lack of published information. Most modern books on the shotgun devote no more than a page or two to the topic.[1]

One suspects that the reason that relatively little has been put down in print about the detail of gunfitting is because a certain mystery, and not a little confusion, surrounds the whole subject. The purpose of these notes – which bear witness to my own quest to understand gunfit more deeply – is to wipe some of the mystery and confusion away and to provide both amateurs and professionals with a useful and straightforward guide. All of this is not to say that the science of gunfit is easily understood, or the craft of gunfitting easily mastered. Far from it. To truly understand gunfit takes years of work; one must understand the basic variables – length, pitch, cast and drop – *and* one must understand their interrelationship. In this, they remind me of nothing so much as Professor Rubic's famous cube!

Just to add to the fun and frustration there are different, often equally valid, solutions to the same gunfitting problems. For example: if one wants to lower the point of impact of a particular gun the normal route would be to increase the drop measurement – i.e. make the stock more crooked in the vertical plane. But one might also increase the cast, change the pitch or raise the rib (or, if it is a single barrelled gun, bend the barrel down). All these things can cause the mean point of impact to be lowered. Confused? Hopefully not (if you are, don't worry – all will be revealed in the forthcoming chapters). Meantime, I emphasise that no mere book is going to turn anyone into an expert gunfitter: only years of practice, based on a foundation of sound knowledge, can do that. Apart from providing a practical guide to the subject, a related, and admittedly ambitious, aim of this book is to establish gunfitting as more of a science than it is at present. I say this in spite of my respect for the traditional gunfitter and his methods, and accepting that it will never be possible to reduce gunfitting to an absolute set of formulae. Nevertheless, I believe the whole subject needs a clearer theoretical footing than it currently has, both to help to teach people to be better gunfitters, and also to explore the limits of human performance with the shotgun. Shooters today, like other sportsmen, are more thoughtful and, for better or worse, more competitive than their predecessors. If we want to improve the design of our gun stocks – I am not a member of the school which believes the evolution of the shotgun stopped in 1880 – we must have a starting point for discussion in which the terms we use are properly defined, and the development and use of our equipment methodically considered. There is a need for more objectivity and less prejudice. Why does one fitter suggest a longer stock than another for the same person? Or more cast? This book sets out to discover answers to such questions: the apparent contradictions are not always what they seem.

Meanwhile, the present somewhat confused state of affairs has a few unhappy consequences, not least the perpetuation in some quarters of an 'ignorance is bliss' attitude towards gunfit (and certain other important aspects of shotgun technology and technique). There are some saloon bar 'experts' who will react to any mention of gunfit with comments like: 'Gunfit? ... Waste of time ... I never bothered ... and I can shoot all right.' Well, this book is not written for such sages; but we might note in passing that most members of the gunfit-is-rubbish lobby have in fact acquired relatively well fitting guns by accident or intuition.

Gunfit *is* important to good shooting, vitally important, and this is as good a place as any to explain why. Although there may be hundreds of stories of people shooting brilliantly with badly fitted guns (most experienced shots can shoot tolerably well with most guns), common sense should also tell us that it will be easier to shoot with a gun that fits – i.e., a gun that can be mounted comfortably, controls recoil effectively, and when mounted properly, shoots towards or just above where one is looking.

The well-designed and well-fitted gun handles more easily under all circumstances, requires less adaptation of the body, and becomes an especially significant advantage when one is tired or off form – part of the reason why people are willing to spend tens of thousands of pounds on the products of Purdey, Boss and Holland & Holland. Some may still say that the good shot can shoot with anything, but even the most brilliant shots – the likes of John Bidwell, who can shoot a good round of skeet with an upside down pump gun held with the butt against his hip – will be able to shoot better with a gun that suits their physical stature and normal shooting style. Perhaps more to the point, many average shots have their performance improved out of all recognition when they have their guns properly fitted.

Of course, gunfit is not the answer to all shooting problems: it is no cure for bad technique or poor mental discipline. Concentrating upon gunfit too much, or upon any other technical aspect of shooting, can negatively affect performance by diverting the focus of one's energy away from the target. The sensible shot strives to find a balance. He or she will recognise the importance of gunfit, sort it out in methodical fashion, but will not become distracted by it either.

Readers may be curious as to where all the information in this book has come from. A good deal of it is the product of my own experience as a shooting instructor and gunfitter, but much has also been contributed by friends and acquaintances working in the same field. The overwhelming generosity of people like Richard Ford, Andrew Perkins and Alan Rhone is noted in the acknowledgements. I might also note that the completion of this project has required several years of specific research and experiment-ation – rather more than initially contemplated. During this time a large number of good gunstocks have been bent, carved, built up and otherwise abused in the pursuit of knowledge!

The original drafts of this book have been carved up in similar fashion. What I present here is not perfect, it is the best book I can write at the moment. I am still learning. Nevertheless, I have decided to publish it now, warts and all, because I think it has reached the stage where it will be useful to others. There may be disagreement on some points, but I am confident that my gunfitting peers would agree with the vast majority of what is presented here (with the possible exception of some of my views on cast). Indeed, I suspect a few may suggest that I have put rather too many trade secrets in print.

A few words, now, on the structure of this volume: the first three chapters – Part 1 – are about the history of stock design and gunfit. Of necessity, these are somewhat simplified: if not, they would end up being several books in themselves. Nevertheless, the information in the first three chapters is important because it puts modern gunfitting and stock design into perspective. In places, this discussion is quite tech-nical; readers not familiar with words like 'cast', 'drop' and 'pitch' may find it useful to read Chapter 4 first, which defines basic terms. Chapter 1 starts with consideration of how the shape of the modern gunstock evolved. Chapters 2 and 3 continue with the theme of history and de-velopment. The chapters which follow – Part 2 – deal with the theory and mechanics of gun fit. They should not require much, if any, prior knowledge to be intelligible, though they are, purposefully, quite con-centrated. I wanted to concentrate the basic principles into as little space as possible.

Finally, I feel honour bound to inform readers that gunfit is, as Brian Hebditch once observed, one of those 'simple but complicated' areas of enquiry where a little knowledge can definitely be a very dangerous thing. Do not fool yourself: if you want to explore this subject you must expect to make mistakes. The wise will experiment with stocks of no great value and always remember the three golden rules of gun fit:

1) Be Methodical.
2) Be Cautious.
3) Be Patient.

Above all else, they will persevere. Acquiring the skills to create a well fitted gun is worth the effort: the knowledge can transform unhappy shooters into happy ones, and ordinary guns into tools every bit as effective as those bespoke works of art made by the world's master gunmakers.

MICHAEL YARDLEY
*London, January 1993*

NOTE

1   I note amongst the honourable exceptions, Robert Arthur's *The Shotgun Stock*, John Brindle's *Shotgun Shooting: Techniques and Technology* and Bruck Bowlen's *Orvis Wingshooting Handbook* – all three books emanating from North America and all of which consider gunfit in detail. There is also important information on gunfitting in the works of Gough Thomas, Chris Craddock, Stanbury and Carlisle, Arthur Hearn, Robert Churchill and, more recently, in Ken Davies's book *The Better Shot*.

# PART ONE

# The History of Gun Design and Stock Fit

---

# 1

## THE EARLY GUN STOCK

The very earliest handguns were nothing more than miniature cannons; the first record of their existence in Europe occurs in the middle of the four-teenth century. The iron, brass or bronze barrels of the early 'handgones' or 'handgunnes' were, if they had any sort of separate stock, typically fastened to straight pieces of wood. In some cases these early stocks were no more than poles which were attached to the barrel by means of a socket or spike at the breech; in others a plank or beam was used, and the barrel attached to it by means of iron rings.

The gunstock at this stage was effectively little more than a tiller (early guns are sometimes referred to as 'gunnis cum telar' – guns with handles – in contemporary manuscripts). The rudimentary stock helped to direct the muzzle of a gun which was often fired from a rest. As far as the human factor was concerned, we can see from early illustrations that the stocks of early longarms were sometimes held against the rib cage, sometimes under the armpit, and sometimes were rested on top of the shoulder.

By the late fifteenth century, the manner in which guns were used had changed significantly. The stock – by now nearly all variations on the beam concept because this design was more comfortable to use and could easily accommodate a gun lock – had become shorter, and developed 'drop' (a downward deviation of the top line of the stock from that of the barrel) to facilitate aiming. However, these stocks were not necessarily designed for support from the shoulder in the modern manner. In Germany in the six-teenth century, a rather lumpy and very short type of stock had become common, designed for shooting from the cheek without any extra support save that from the hands. Such stocks did not control recoil very well, but they allowed fairly precise aiming. They became popular elsewhere in Europe, and remained in use in Germany on target rifles well into the eighteenth century. The influence of 'German' stock is still to be seen on those European and American sporting arms which have an exaggerated cheek piece. Meantime in France the petronel stock emerged. It had a very pronounced downward curve and was designed for firing with the butt resting low on the chest. The name petronel is derived from the French *poitrine* meaning breast, itself derived from the Latin *pectus*.

Early gun stocks might be held on top of the shoulder, under the armpit, or rested against the check without support from the front of the shoulder or chest.

## Origins of the Modern Stock

By the beginning of the seventeenth century gun stocks designed to be used in the modern manner – with support from the chest and/or shoulder and with the cheek or side of the jaw resting upon the comb – had become predominant. Perhaps the most common type of stock for heavy military longarms of the late sixteenth/early seventeenth centuries was the 'fish-tail' design. This was a heavy and sometimes elaborate affair which typically had concave top and bottom edges to its butts, a deep butt sole and a distinct thumb groove which made it easier to both hold and to aim (the groove took the thumb out of the line of sight).

The fish-tail stock was an improvement on most earlier types, offering better control of recoil (vital for increasingly powerful military weapons) as

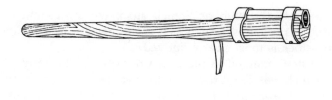

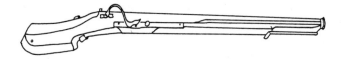

The development of the gun stock. *(top to bottom)*: pole stock, beam stock, sixteenth-century stock with shaped butt and drop, fishtail stock, club stock

well as improving aim, but it was still clumsy, and quite unsuited to any purpose where really rapid movements of the gun might be required such as in wing-shooting.[1] Enter the 'club' or 'French' stock, which was much more suited to sporting applications, and which is the design from which the modern shotgun stock is most clearly derived.

The design had first emerged in the Low Countries in the early seventeenth century, which was about the same time as the first locks using the flint and steel principle appeared. The combination of the shoulder butt and more efficient locks made wingshooting a far more practical possibility. The stock acquired its Gallic epithet because it was popularised by French gunmakers who published books on gun design which were widely distributed in Europe and beyond. By the late seventeenth century, it had become very widely copied and refined. Usually the club stock had a straight, fairly thick grip of circular cross section (modern straight-grip guns tend to be quite narrow and oval or diamond in cross section), considerable drop at heel, combined with a very rounded heel, a pronounced bump just beneath it and considerable pitch down. The stock also tended to be very thick, especially towards its bottom edge, and rather shorter than most modern gun stocks. However, the overall length of guns was much longer than today with barrels of 4 ft length being typical. Guns of this era were also full stocked, that is typically the woodwork extended to the muzzles. Later, the early form of the club stock developed into the 'hand rail' stock. In this form, both the wrist (the grip area) and the comb were sharply defined; the wrist had an exaggerated cylindrical form extending into the mass of the butt, the comb was flat-sided and narrow towards the breech. The hand rail stock – so named because the wrist of it looked like a rail – was the final stage in the evolution of the modern sporting gun stock. The latter was born in the late eighteenth century when the wrist and comb were blended into their modern form. It was at about the same time that the practice of scoring or chequering at the wrist and forestock to improve grip became common.

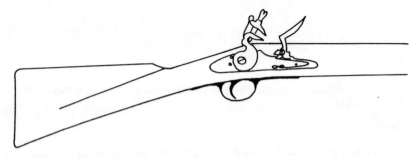

The hand rail form of the gun stock.

### The First Fitted Guns

Although there are odd examples of German cheek stock guns which have been bent in the manner of a modern crossover stock, gunfitting in the modern sense probably began with the club stock. The firearms curators at the Royal Armouries at the Tower of London have recently been able to examine nine sporting guns acquired by the Dukes of Brunswick around 1700. These guns, made by various craftsmen, are all fowling pieces, and all have club type stocks; some are of the crossover type, some are cast on, some cast off. They have clearly been made to fit either individuals or, at the least (and far less likely), specific types of shooter, viz., right-handers with left master eyes, left-handers with left master eyes and right-handers with right master eyes. Furthermore, all of the Brunswick guns appear to be unmodified (the tangs of the butt plate, trigger guard and breech all follow the centre line of the stock although it is not straight, i.e. they were almost certainly made originally with cast. This would seem to provide clear evidence of gunfit being taken seriously by certain gunsmiths and some discerning customers by 1700. However, the guns in the Royal Armouries do not show, being special weapons made for a noble house, that a sophisticated consideration of gunfit was universal at that time; all the indications are that it was not.

The club stock became the standard stock for all military and sporting longarms, and was refined throughout the eighteenth century via the hand rail form discussed earlier. It became, as it evolved, less bulky and less bulbous. As the stock narrowed, its sides also became flatter. The shape of the heel was modified to make it more comfortable and secure at the shoulder. The wrist became longer, and better blended into the rest of the stock. Typically, the club stock had a straight grip, but some Continental makers produced something very like the modern semi-pistol shape by incorporating a carving of a bird's head at the bottom rear of the wrist. Although these additions were decorative, they also had a practical function (at least when well conceived) to improve the right hand's grip, and with it muzzle control.

Until the early eighteenth century, continental gunmakers had led the way in sporting firearms design. But during the eighteenth century, British craftsmen, who had once lagged behind their cousins in Europe, were producing work of exceptional quality and design. By the close of the century, British gunmakers were producing shotguns as fine as any in the world; perhaps not as gaudy as the best Continental products, but often better engineered and more practically stocked. English gunmakers were particularly instrumental in further developing the anti-recoil properties of the stock, a feature of design which became more important as makers like Henry Nock improved ballistic performance.[2]

The introduction of Nock's breech, not to mention the major improvements in gunpowder in the late eighteenth and early nineteenth century, had a very significant effect on gun design. Because the propellant charge was burnt more efficiently, barrel length could be reduced. Before the patent breech, fowling guns typically had barrels of 40 in. or more; now 34,

32 or even 30 in. was all that was needed to ensure adequate combustion (which also made double-barrelled guns a practical possibility). Stocks changed as well. The traditional full stock to the muzzles gave way to the more elegant, and lighter, half stock. The shape of the butt evolved. Higher velocity weapons recoiled more; a sloping butt aggravated the problem. Moreover, a butt which was much inclined at the comb was not suited to a faster handling gun; it was awkward to bring up to face and shoulder quickly and made shots at high birds difficult.

## NOTES

1   Wingshooting – shooting at flying birds – is first documented in a German manuscript of 1560, but it may have been common in some parts of Europe well before this date. The first illustration relating to wingshooting was published by Giacomo Franco in 1609. Even the Japanese *Book of Firearms* shows that the technique was practised on those islands before 1612. However, it appears that the English were a rather backward lot as far as the new sport was concerned. They had long potted sitting birds with firearms loaded with 'hayle' shot – a practice which had been legislated against without much success since the fifteenth century – but 'shooting flying' did not really catch on in these isles until the late seventeenth century; it appears to have been popularised in England by the courtiers of Charles II, who brought the sport, together with the equipment to pursue it, from fashionable France. Samuel Pepys mentions it in his famous diaries; by 1688 Richard Blome informs us in his *Gentleman's Recreations*, '. . . it is now the mode to shoot flying.' Wingshooting rapidly established itself in England: during the eighteenth century a number of books appeared – *The Young Sportsman's Instructor* (Gervase Markham, 1712), *Pteryplegia: Or the Art of Shooting Flying* (George Markland, 1727), *The Art of Shooting Flying* (Thomas Page, 1766), *An Essay on Shooting* (Anon., 1789). By 1792 *The Sportsman's Directory* could note, '. . . the rage for shooting flying was never at a higher pitch than at present'.

2   Nock's great improvement to the flintlock gun was his 'patent breech' of 1787, which combined a chamber in the breech plug with an ante-chamber drilled crosswise from the barrel touch-hole and closed on the other side with a screw-plug. Pollard's *History of Firearms* notes, '. . . With the powder loosely confined in this ante-chamber, the flash from the pan produced an explosion rather than simple burning. Flame was thus transferred from the ante-chamber to the chamber proper and on to the propellant charge almost instantly. So rapid were the successive explosions, in fact, that they sounded like one. The time lapse of the older chambered breech was eliminated . . . '(Pollard's *History of Firearms*, p 144, Country Life Books, 1983.)

# 2

# GUNFIT: THE MODERN ERA

During the late eighteenth century, a vital sporting firearms industry and the fashion for scientific or pseudo-scientific method, stimulated writers across Europe to consider guns and shooting far more technically than in the past (previously it had been considered ungentlemanly to consider technical aspects of firearms in detail). Gunfit, amongst many other topics, began to be considered more systematically. In 1789, the anonymous (but probably English) author of *An Essay on Shooting* recorded:

> Every Sportsman has his own manner of bringing his gun up to his shoulder, and each follows his own fancy with respect to the stock of his fowling piece, and its shape. Some like it short, others long; one prefers it straight another bent ... And although there are some sportsmen, who shoot equally well with pieces stocked in different ways and shapes, yet certain principles may be laid down, as well upon what is the proper length, as upon the proper degree of bent, that the stock of a gun should have. Generally speaking ... it is certain that for a tall, long-armed man, the stock of a gun should be longer than for one of lesser stature, and shorter arm.
>
> That a straight stock is proper for he whom who has high shoulders, and a short neck; for if it were much bent, it would be very difficult for him, especially at the quick motion required in shooting at a flying or running object, to place the butt of the gun-stock firmly to the shoulder. On the contrary, a man with low shoulders, and a long neck, requires a stock much bent; for if it is straight, he will, in the act of lowering his head to the part of the stock at which his cheek should rest, in taking aim, feel a constraint, which he never experiences, when by the effect of the proper degree of bent, the stock lends him some assistance, and, as it were, meets his aim half way.[1]

The comments from *An Essay on Shooting* show a fairly deep understanding of several aspects of gunfit in the second half of the eighteenth century, and have been included here for that reason. Nevertheless, it would be wrong to see them, or the Brunswick guns mentioned in Chapter 1 as an indication of a widespread understanding of gunfit amongst any significant number of eighteenth-century sportsmen. It was probably not until the second quarter of the nineteenth century that the importance of gunfit became more generally appreciated. With all the technical developments in locks, barrels and powder which led to shorter ignition times and more consistent ballistics, standards of marksmanship rose, and subtleties in gun design became apparent that might have been missed before.

Joe Manton, the inventive London gunmaker credited as being 'the father of modern gunmaking' and promoter, amongst many other things, of the elevated sighting rib,[2] particularly understood the importance of precise gunfitting and offered his customers shotguns made to suit both their physique and shooting style. In 1834, his celebrated customer, Lieutenant Colonel Peter Hawker, wrote in *Instructions to Young Sportsmen*: 'The length, bend and casting off of a stock, must, of course, be fitted to the shooter, who should have his measure for them as carefully entered on a gunmaker's books, as that for a suit of clothes on those of his tailor.'

Not every shooter of the period would have been able to afford the luxury of a bespoke gun by a first class maker like Manton; most, as today, would have merely picked the best gun on the shelf (an economical method of gunfitting which still has much to recommend it), perhaps having it modified slightly after purchase. Nevertheless, in the years following the publication of Hawker's commercially successful *Instructions to Young Sportsmen*, shooters and gunmakers became far more aware of the importance of gunfit.

Another factor stimulating interest in the subject was the development of increasingly specialised shooting sports during the nineteenth century. One which offered significant financial rewards to the owner of a well fitted gun was live pigeon shooting. Indeed, the development of pigeon shooting from traps, which gave its name to the modern sport of 'trap' shooting at clay pigeons, gave great impetus to many different aspects of shotgunning – gunfit, powder development, and (from the 1870s) choke boring. Huge sums of money were wagered on the results of pigeon matches at Hurlingham and other clubs when the sport reached its zenith in the mid–1800s. And with large sums at stake, it was hardly surprising that there should have been a great deal of speculation on just what the ideal characteristics of a good pigeon shooting gun should be. There seemed agreement on two points. Pigeon shooting guns should be made heavier than 'game' guns, and higher in the stock so that they might throw their shot high to meet a rising target.[3]

The introduction of breech loading shotguns – first the pinfires in the 1840s and 50s, then central fire weapons in the 60s and 70s – was another profound influence on the design of the modern gunstock. The new guns – which did not suffer from the problem of flashing pans or 'spitting' percussion caps – made possible a less upright head position. Thus, the need for pronounced bend was further reduced: a less upright shooting style tends to bring the shooter's centre of gravity forward and lower the position of the eye in relation to the top of the breech/barrel. Moreover, the weight of the early breechloaders (makers tended to veer on the side of caution when

The Holland & Holland Shooting School at the turn of the century.

making the mechanism of the new guns) was yet another factor which may have popularised guns with less drop. Heavy guns, especially heavy long barrelled side-by-sides, can shoot low.

The popularity of pigeon shooting from traps and the advent of the breechloader were far from the only factors influencing the development of the British shotgun and its stock in the nineteenth century. The fad for driven game shooting which was evident from about 1870 also had a profound effect on gun and stock design. Several Anglo-centric authorities would say that driven game shooting was *the* influence on the design and development of the sporting shotgun. The technique of driven shooting was different to traditional 'walked up' quarry shooting. The eighteenth-century/early nineteenth-century style of shooting is seen in contemporary sporting prints. The stance is very wide – typically a wide pace and edge on to the target: just what one would expect of someone who is walking with a gun and suddenly flushes game. Driven game shooters, on the other hand, were assigned positions facing the area to be beaten; the natural tendency in these circumstances was to adopt a stance with the feet closer together. There was still individual variation – some favoured an oblique stance; others preferred to be almost square to the target – but both types of stance, and all the variations in between, take the shoulder upon which the gun is mounted further away from the eye/target line than the older edge-on styles. Unless the head is tilted over to one side, alteration of the stock in the horizontal plane was required to bring the eye back in line with the rib. This change of style is one likely reason why guns of the last quarter of the nineteenth century are notably more cast than those made earlier. There may also be an element of fashion encouraged by the twin cults of gunfitting and driven game shooting. According to traditional British gunfitting lore, the cast gun facilitates the firing of the gun as soon as it touches the shoulder without the need to adjust the head position to achieve the correct barrel target relationship.'[4]

Driven shooting, like pigeon shooting, and the demise of the flintlock and percussion guns, was yet another factor encouraging the use of guns with less drop; it may also account for the exaggerated toe on many English guns. Where targets are rising and/or being driven to the shooter's front, a little less drop equals a little more built-in lead. On high quartering and crossing targets, less drop and more toe can help one keep on the line of the bird.

A gun with a fairly straight stock relative to the bore axis has another distinct advantage for the driven game shot: it reduces felt recoil. There was a very real need for this quality in a gun. The bags could be astonishing. In fifty-one years of shooting Colonel Hawker shot 17,753 head of game; by 1900 Lord de Grey had already killed over 300,000 birds at an average of over 10,000 a year or 200 a week (by the time of his death in 1923 de Grey, by then the Marquess of Ripon, had a lifetime bag of 556,000!). A sportsman who shot this much in a year, often with lightly built pairs and trios of guns, had to have a gun and a shooting technique which kept recoil to a minimum. How was this achieved? As far as stocks were concerned, by a new emphasis both on good gunfitting and practical design. It is a notable feature of the late Victorian game gun that, apart from having modest drop, it usually had a considerable taper towards the front of the comb on the butt – thus removing wood which might otherwise smack into the cheekbone as the gun recoiled back.

### The Cult Of Gunfit

As the great shots indulged in their passion for shooting, the spirit of mechanical invention and innovation so characteristic of their era ensured that much more thought was given to the theoretical principles which governed the manufacture and the use of sporting firearms. The great names of the London gun trade continued the fight to become number one and win the custom of the likes of de Grey and Walsingham.

The famous firm of Purdey built their reputation on guns which were superbly made, elegant and, perhaps their greatest selling point, superbly fitted. In 1900 G.T. Teasdale-Buckell noted in *Experts on Guns and Shooting*, 'Mr Purdey will tell you that very early in his business career he began to make a speciality of fitting customers with their stocks. His father had a gun with an alterable stock as far back as he could remember, and probably much further, but fitting had not been made such a study of as he thought it deserved to be, and that he henceforth made of it, with considerable

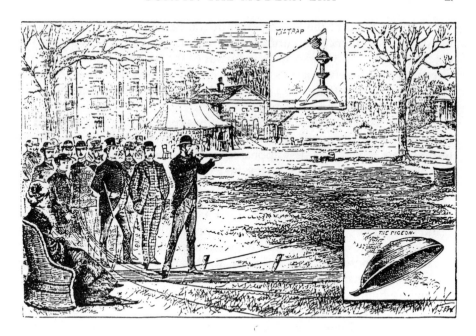

'Terracota pigeon' shooting demonstration at Ranelagh Club, London,
10 March 1883.

success, so that for the greater part of the last fifty years, a very large number
of the best shots at home and abroad have been through his hands.'

By the 1890s, nearly all the great makers had opened their own 'shooting
schools'. Charles Lancaster was one of the first (and included amongst his
clients Annie Oakley). Shooting grounds had existed previously however.
Teasdale-Buckell notes that Joseph Lang had opened one in 1827 for practice
gun testing and fitting, but the new shooting schools offered instruction in
the right style and a new and hitherto unattainable fitting service based on
the 'skeleton' or 'try gun' as invented by W.P. Jones of Birmingham.[5] The
development of the shooting school also coincided with the appearance of
the clay pigeon.[6] It allowed the schools to simulate all manner of game birds,
not least the celebrated, almost venerated, 'High Pheasant'. We might also
note that the introduction of the clay target started an argument which still
rages. Do clays provide useful practice for game shooting? Most instructors
experienced in both game and clay shooting would say yes, subject to the
proviso that the clays were presented in the right way. There are limitations
to the clay target, they slow down as they fly and they fall. To make clays
really useful practice for live quarry is always a test of imagination and skill
for instructors.

As the shooting schools of the great makers and their imitators prospered, the shooting press of the late nineteenth and early twentieth century was full of correspondence on gunfit and the virtues and vices of try guns for determining it. Most voices were in favour of the try gun; however, W.W. Greener stated sagely that try guns were limited in their usefulness because of their peculiar balance, and concluded, that in anything but the most expert hands, they were a gimmick.[7]

One firm which did (and do) offer a truly expert service was Holland & Holland. They were sufficiently proud of their expertise to republish testimonials which had first appeared in the shooting press. A Holland brochure produced just before the first war quotes 'Quite Satisfied' and 'Proper Fit', correspondents to *The Field*:

> *Quite Satisfied*: 'Sir . . . For some time I had been convinced that my gun did not suit me, though assured of the contrary by two first-class London makers, to one of whose grounds I went to shoot. I had the stock altered exactly as shown by the Try Gun at Messrs. HOLLANDS' Shooting Grounds, Kensal Rise, with the result that my shooting was at once immensely improved . . . '
>
> *Proper Fit*: 'In shooting I never found that the gun came up quite to my liking . . . This I never could account for until last July I went to Messrs. HOLLAND & HOLLAND'S shooting grounds and used their Try Gun. A few shots told me my that my left eye was the 'master eye', and that I did not want quite so much bend on my stock, and not quite so short. I had one of my guns altered to these requirements, and have since had the satisfaction of improving my shooting fifty percent. The gun comes up well, and I can shoot with the greatest ease and confidence.'

Try guns were improved as the new century progressed. Arthur Hearn writing in the late 1930s notes that whilst there were many good gunmakers, 'there seem to be few really experienced gunfitters, and some of these are using obsolete "try guns" that have only one movement for cast-off and cast-on; thus where cast-off is needed one gets too much where it is not wanted, i.e. at the heel, thus putting the stock on the arm or on the point of the shoulder, which is just where it ought not to be, and very little on the face of the stock, which is really the place that counts.' Hearn also defines what he considers a 'modern' try gun: 'The most modern "try gun" has every movement, and in the hands of an experienced fitter any shaped stock, from perfectly straight [here meaning without cast] to fully cross-eyed from either shoulder may be arrived at.'[8]

Although there was, as there remains, considerable argument on the details of individual gunfit and stock design, by about 1880 the beautiful form of the classic English game gun had become fairly fixed (it still owed much to Manton). In his classic work *The Modern Sportsman's Gun and Rifle*, published

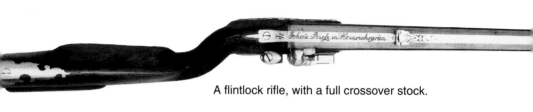

A flintlock rifle, with a full crossover stock.

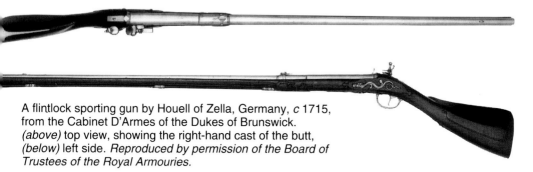

A flintlock sporting gun by Houell of Zella, Germany, c 1715,
from the Cabinet D'Armes of the Dukes of Brunswick.
(above) top view, showing the right-hand cast of the butt,
(below) left side. Reproduced by permission of the Board of
Trustees of the Royal Armouries.

A group of London-made early nineteenth-century sporting
guns. (top to bottom) by John Manton, c 1800; by Alexander
Wilson, c 1815; by John Manton, c 1813; and by James
Purdey, c 1820. Reproduced by permission of the Board of
Trustees of the Royal Armouries.

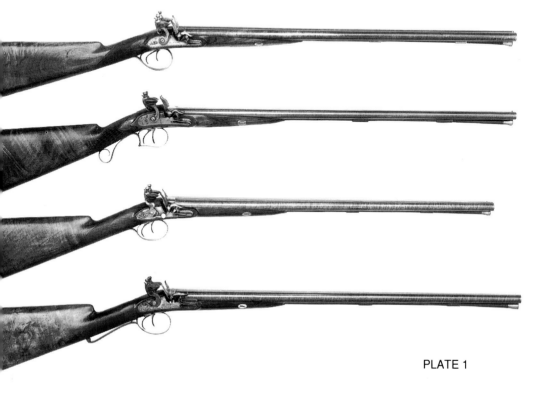

PLATE 1

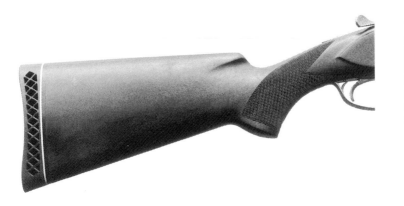

The stock of a modern Browning trap gun. Note the full pistol grip, the relatively thick comb with flutes at the nose of the cone, and a ventilated recoil pad.

The stock of a Beretta over-and-under game gun. Note the pistol grip, this time combined with an elegantly tapered comb.

A Miroku 6000 trap gun. Note the raised rib and the parallel comb.

A Perazzi MX8DG2. This gun has a very pronounced pistol grip reminiscent of the style made popular by the famous American shooter, Rudy Etchen. Also note the adjustable trigger.

PLATE 2

in 1882, J.H. Walsh, then editor of *The Field*, set out the 'usual measurements' of the English sporting gun:

| | |
|---|---|
| From front trigger to middle of heel | 14½ (inches) |
| From front trigger to middle of toe | 14¾ |
| From comb to machine [to the line of the rib] | 1½ |
| From heel to machine [as above] | 2 |
| Cast-off at toe | ⅜ |
| Cast off at heel | ³⁄₁₆ |

Walsh might have added that at the middle of the butt sole, the stock would generally have been around 1⅞ in. wide, and, at the grip, about 1⅛ in. The depth of butt at sole would have been about 5¼ in., and at the grip – measured from the back of the top strap through to the back of the trigger guard – about 1½ in.

How do these figures compare to the guns of today?

The typical game gun today is a little longer in the stock: Walsh's dimensions would equate to a length of about 14¹/₂ in. to the middle of the butt plate; a modern English sporting gun with double triggers would, typically, be around 14¹/₂ in. to the middle for the mythical average man (though 'shelf' guns may be made longer), with an ¹/₈ in. extra to bump and ¹/₄ or ³/₈ in. extra to toe. The modern trend is towards a less protruding toe. Typical Victorian dimensions would have been ¹/₄ in. to bump/heel and ¹/₂ or ⁵/₈ in. to toe (Purdey still prefer a long toe, ¹/₂ in. is their norm with ¹/₈ in. to bump).

Drop measurements remain very similar, 1½ in. comb and 2 in. at heel would still be considered very standard. Cast remains similar too (although extremes of cast are less common), an ¹/₈ or ³/₁₆ in. at heel, with ¹/₄ or ⁵/₁₆ in. at toe, would be typical. The dimensions relating to grip and stock thickness are similar. The classic English or Scottish game gun still has a thin, straight grip: 4⅛ in. is a typical circumference measurement. The depth of butt sole has not changed much either, and the comb of the modern game gun is still tapered like a Victorian gun but it is often thinner, especially in the middle. I suspect the change relates more to aesthetics than functional improvement.[9]

What about today's over-and-unders, Brownings, Berettas and the like? How do they compare to the game guns of Walsh's day? At least as far as the field, skeet and sporting models are concerned, they share similar general dimensions, but there are some significant differences too. For example, although stock length of the modern mass-made over-and-under is very similar at first sight to the Victorian English gun, it should be noted that most mass-produced over-and-unders are equipped with single triggers, so their stock measurements actually equate to a double trigger gun about ¼ in. longer, thus confirming the trend, in all shotguns designed for the British market anyway, towards longer stocks. As with modern game guns, butt sole depth remains about the same, 5⅛ in. would be typical. Grips of mass-made over-and-unders are nearly always of the pistol pattern because they are thought to suit the now perfected single trigger mechanism. They are considerably thicker on average than the dainty straight grips of Victorian guns and their modern copies (a typical pistol grip on a modern over-and-under will be about 4¾ in. in girth). Combs on the machine-made over-and-unders do not usually show as much taper as the Victorian guns but do tend to be quite thick but without the careful shaping of the Victorian bench-made stock. Modern over-and-unders also tend to have less cast than English guns of the late Victorian era, indeed many have none at all.

Greener's Rational Gun Stock.

## The Rational Stock

Though beautiful and functional, the classic English stock shape was not to everybody's taste. W.W. Greener, who studied his subject most carefully, presented the Rational Gun Stock, and considered its advantages in his famous work *The Gun and its Development*. The rational stock had more drop at heel than the typical late Victorian English stock, moreover it combined a semi pistol grip with an unusually shaped comb. Greener writes:

'In this stock . . . there is more than the usual bend at the bump or heel, and the comb is not straight, but arched slightly; and as the cheek touches the stock about midway between the heel and the thumb, it is there, and there only, that the stock need be straight . . . .With the usual English gun-stock, put up in the usual manner, it will be found that about one quarter of the butt projects above [W.W is slightly over-stating his case], and has no bearing against the shoulder. This leaves the sharp narrow toe to steady the gun and to take the recoil. With the rational stock, the face of the shooter will be resting upon the stock when the bump or heel has reached a level of the shoulder. The bend of the gun will, with the rational stock, be about 2½ in. at heel, 1½ in. at comb, and 1½ in. midway between heel and comb.'

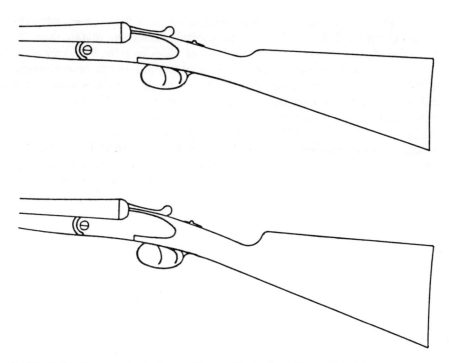

A classic English game stock and Churchill's Natural Stock *(below)*.

## Churchill's Natural Stock

Greener was not the only inventive and commercially-minded gunmaker to suggest improvement upon the classic English stock. A quarter of a century later, another charismatic gunmaker, Robert Churchill, presented his new shape of stock. It was designed to complement his famous 25 in. barrelled 'XXV' guns. Churchill's 'Natural' stock, unlike Greener's 'Rational' stock, still looked familiar and, one suspects, sold rather better because of it. Churchill's theory (and there is certainly some truth in it) was that the traditional gun stock had evolved for reasons of fashion or aesthetics to become rather too straight in the grip. His natural stock is heavily influenced by the roach-bellied stocks of the late flintlock era, for which he had a special fondness. 'The tendency of many modern guns,' he wrote in 1955, 'has been towards a grip which is too straight for practical mounting [too straight a grip tends to make one cock the wrist of the gripping hand, a movement which can cause the swing to be checked]. The line is graceful . . . but it is a handicap in use. The natural stock developed in my short-barrelled guns is the same in bend and general measurements as the last named but with very material alterations to the grip. The tang of the action and trigger plate curve down so that the hand moves naturally parallel to the line of sight without enforcing a sustained position to the right arm.'[10]

Another peculiarity of some Churchill guns is an 'offset comb', whereby the line of the comb is offset so it is more parallel but more distant from the line of the rib, the offset serving to replace, or, more usually, to augment the cast of the stock. One advantage of the offset comb, recently re-introduced by the Beretta firm on some of their 'S.O.' range of sidelock over-and-unders, is that in recoil the stock is not forced into the cheekbone as it can be with a traditionally cast gun.

In recent years in England, few manufacturers have dared to experiment as Greener and Churchill once did (Hollands, Rigby's and McKay Brown are notable exceptions however). Most of the few firms that survive produce guns which have changed little in their form in fifty years. Beautiful and functional though their products may be, it is a pity that the gun trade in Britain has been allowed to stagnate so; development demands risks.

## NOTES

1  *An Essay on Shooting* was first published in Dublin in 1789, and later in the same year, in London. Part of the book was an acknowledged translation of the French work *La Chasse au Fusil* by G-F. Magne de Marolles, first published in Paris in 1781 and in enlarged form in 1788. According to W.S. Curtis, who wrote an introduction to a British reprint (Richmond Publishing Company, 1975), 'In England the Essay opened a floodgate of literature . . . and for some years it was shamelessly plagiarised'.

2  Manton realised that the guns of his era tended to shoot low. To try a find a way to counteract this problem, Manton experimented with various forms of barrel rib. His 1806 patent for the Elevated Rib (later disputed in court) is a fascinating window on the great gunmaker's thinking: 'the top piece or top rib must be made high at the breech ends of the barrels and tapering off to the muzzles. The intention . . . is to give the barrels elevation to throw the centre of the charge of shot up to the object aimed at the distance required. I should recommend the top piece or top rib for general shooting to be made so high above the surface of the barrels at the breech that a double gun will throw the centre of the charge of shot up to the object aimed at the distance of forty yards . . . This elevated top piece or top rib may be made of iron, steel, brass or any metallic or other substance that will answer the purpose, and may be grooved out in the usual manner, or made flat, round or any other shape . . . The advantages of this elevated top piece or rib are, that sportsmen will be less liable to shoot under their game, and the aim will be more direct and less confused, and that a light double gun can be made to throw the middle of its charge of shot up to the object aimed at the distance required and also that it will not be necessary to bend the barrels upwards or to make them clumsy at the breech . . . 'As we will see later in this book ribs are an important consideration in gunfitting because they can effect shot placement quite dramatically. Whether or not he actually invented them, and the evidence is that he did not, we can thank Joe Manton for being the first to really understand their importance.

3  Apart from the extra weight and high combs, the double-barrelled pigeon guns of the late nineteenth and early twentieth centuries would evolve to include flat, file cut ribs rather than the concave type which became the standard on side-by-side game guns, heavily choking, typically full and full, long barrels and half or full pistol grips, often combined with a single trigger.

4   This firing without check was *de rigueur* for the late Victorian game shot and is still considered good form in game shooting circles. For example, 'Shotgunner' (*aka* James Openshaw) noted of the late Sir Joseph Nickerson in the *Shooting News* of 7 October 1988, 'He was shooting in the classic style, as soon as the stock touched his shoulder the gun went off and the bird was killed.' However, I am rather sceptical about the idea that a gun with no cast is slower or more awkward to use *for someone of relatively normal physique* even though the idea was sold to the Victorian game shot and his successors. The importance of shooting as soon as the gun touches the shoulder has been over emphasised. What is really important is that there should be no prolonged tracking of the target with a mounted gun: one should trust the first, the instinctive aim, but one should not shoot carelessly before the muscles of the shoulder have tensed.

5   James Purdey the younger's comment to his son, as reported by Teasdale-Buck-ell, would seem to indicate that the concept of the try gun may be older than we think. Sadly, I can find no other evidence supporting the existence of the early Purdey gun, though there is no reason to doubt its existence. Geoffrey Boothroyd notes 'There are some twenty patents on try guns. The first *effective* one was patented by W.P. Jones ... in 1889. The earliest appears to be Clarke in 1881. These were followed by H.A.A. Thorn [Charles Lancaster] in 1890, then Holland, and Wm. Ford of Birmingham all in the same year.' In trying to find evidence for early try guns I did however come across the measuring cradle of Ezekiel Baker, gunmaker to George IV. This device, built in 1828, now rests within the collection of Royal Armouries at the Tower of London and was created by Baker as a means of ensuring all the King's guns might be adjusted to the same dimensions.

6   The invention of the clay pigeon by George Ligowsky *circa* 1880 (and like so many other shooting inventions it is disputed), also created new sporting possibilities. There had been glass balls since about 1860, and they had been quite popular both for practice and competition. But the appearance of clay pigeons ensured that inanimate target shooting with shotguns would become one of the world's great sports. It became particularly popular as a pastime in the United States (it was already well established there in the 1890s). In Britain, *The Illustrated London News* of 10 March 1883 records a 'Terracotta pigeon' shooting demonstration taking place at Ranelagh Club in London. Ten years later 'The Inanimate Bird Shooting Society' held its first championship in Wimbledon Park. The success of clay pigeon shooting on both sides of the Atlantic, ensured that it would develop its own specialised weaponry, with, of course, their own special gunfit requirements.

7   I have some sympathy for both points, and would note to this day there are no more than a dozen men in the United Kingdom who are real masters of gun fitting by try gun.

8   My experience of try guns, modern and otherwise, is that few have sufficient adjustment to create a fully cross-eyed stock.

9   Purdey still use a fuller comb, I find, that on their pigeon guns is especially comfortable and definitely worthy of imitation.

10   Colonel Hawker made the same point about grip shape a hundred years earlier: 'All stocks should have a good fall in the hand, and not be, as some are, nearly horizontal in that part. This has nothing to do with the general bend or mounting of the stock, but is merely to keep the hand to the natural position ... '

# 3

# DEVELOPMENT OF THE STOCK ABROAD

So far, we have mainly been concerned with the development of the shot-gun stock in Great Britain, but we must also look abroad. In Continental Europe and in the United States today, there is a preference in field guns for shorter stocks – 14 in. might be considered typical – and more drop. As Roland Wild of Holland and Holland Shooting School notes: 'The American style of game shooting is rather different to the British. One must talk in generalities, and, as in Britain, there are a wide variety of individual styles, but, that said, the Americans tend to be rifle oriented. They lack our experi-ence of driven shooting. When using a shotgun, they stand very edge on to the target, and distribute their weight more evenly between their feet than we tend to now. Moreover, when they mount a shotgun they typically have a two stage movement, the first is to bring the gun back to the shoulder, the second to begin the swing. The British, on the other hand, tend to push the gun to the bird in one smooth movement. The British style which is squarer to the target, involves pushing the shoulder up and forward to meet the gun. It requires more cast, more length and less drop.'

Although there are today very distinct differences between British and American shooting styles, American stock design has been notably affected by British and other European traditions. The famous American firearms writer and hunter Jack O'Connor explained in *The Complete Book of Shooting* in 1965:

American stocks for double guns were influenced both by the British and by the Germans, but more pistol grips were used than straight grips and in the higher grades American checkering and decoration tended to look more like the German than the British ... trapshooting and skeet have affected stock design in the United States, and a fairly early development in trapshooting was the beavertail forend, a large flat forend which kept the trapshooter's hand away from the hot barrels and gave him a greater degree of control over his gun ... The American market has largely been taken over by the automatic (self-loading) and pump shotguns, and even these have been redesigned to lend themselves to mass production with a minimum of hand labour. Almost all of these American repeaters are made with pistol grip butt stocks, rather large forends to house repeating mechanisms if the guns are automatics or to serve as slide handles if the guns are pumps. All American shotgun stocks have thicker and more rounded combs than do most European guns.'

O'Connor also has some interesting things to say on the measurements of American guns:

> American stock dimensions are just about the same: Length of pull for a field gun, 14 inches; drop at comb from 1½ to 1⅝ inches; drop at heel, 2½ inches [these would still be typical measurements for many American made guns]. These are the dimensions of a reasonably straight stock [meaning one without abnormal drop] and they are a pretty good compromise. Anyone from 5 feet 8 inches to 6 feet 1 inch can adjust himself to one of these standard American stocks and make a pretty good stab at shooting it ... These dimensions started coming along in the early years of this century. In the 1880s and 1890s, stocks were much more 'crooked', had much more drop at comb and heel. Some old guns had 2 inches or more drop at comb and 3½ inches or more drop at heel. Apparently the old-timers who used them were a stiff-necked lot who hated to bend their heads. These old crooked-stocked guns were slow to point and tended to pattern low. If shot with heavy loads they kicked like the devil.

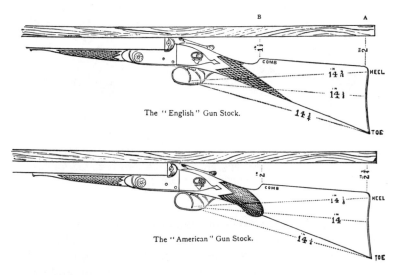

Greener's illustration of English and American gun stocks c 1900.

O'Connor's observations dovetail well with W.W.Greener's comments on American guns which were published more than half a century earlier: 'Americans use guns with stocks much more crooked, as when shooting they keep the head erect, and many English colonists follow this rule, the crooked gun stock being common in South Africa and Australia.'[1]

If any more confirmation were needed, we might look to the legendary American Shooter, Adam Bogardus, who wrote in the 1870s in his *Field*,

*Cover and Trap Shooting*, 'I choose a stock of moderate length and one that is rather crooked – one with a drop of about three inches. This sort of gun comes even up to the shoulder with most men, and you do not have to crook the neck much in taking aim with it.' Bogardus goes on to describe his rifle-like shooting style, which involved taking deliberate aim along the rib – a technique he thought essential for consistent shooting. Rifle influenced, American shotgunners still tend to be more deliberate aimers than their UK counterparts.

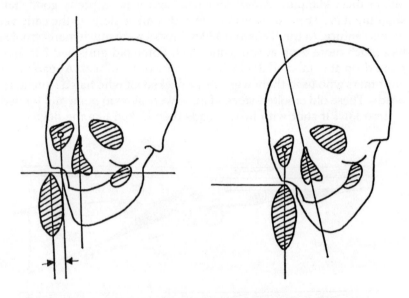

This diagram shows the different head positions required for cast and uncast stocks (after Gough Thomas).

American stocks, old and new, are not just shorter and more crooked than British ones: stocks emanating from the United States usually have no cast.[2] Their extra drop allows the shooter to get his/her eye in line with the rib by a cant or turn of the head against the comb. Many British (and indeed some American) authorities would say that cast-less guns, which require a movement of the head to bring the eye in line with the rib, are a disadvantage, but one is minded to look at the extraordinary scores of some US skeet and trap shooters who use such weapons. Who is going to tell the man who shoots 500 or more birds straight – as some top US skeet and trap shooters have done – that his gun doesn't fit! One reason why American competition shooters succeed with castless guns may be their more deliberate shooting style as described earlier, on the other hand, it may just be that cast is not that important for most people. Less contentiously, few would argue with the proposition that a deliberate, rifle-like style, where one consciously aims along the rib for every shot, makes cast a less important consideration because one is making a constant check on the eye/rib/target relationship (which is not to suggest I advocate such a technique).

## Italy

Whilst mentioning national differences and innovations, we might also make special note of the Italians. Until quite recently, their trap shooters were fond of shooting very square to the target, with the gun mounted very much lower than the British. This sort of style required a gun with more drop: like the Americans, but for different reasons. Many Italians still appear to like a lower mount than is popular in Britain and with it bend their necks far more forward than would be advised here. The Italians also appear to like far fatter combs on their stocks than the rest of us. They tend to roll their heads on to the stock rather than to bring the stock up to the face as is considered good form in Britain.

Italian shooting customs and gun design, like those in the USA, may look slightly odd to British eyes, but Italy is without doubt one of the great shooting countries of the world. The Italians have been most dynamic in the field of shotgun design in recent years. They are the kings of the mass-produced shotgun market and they are particular experts in the field of trapshooting (which with over a million participants is one of the most popular sports in Italy).

Beretta, Perazzi and Franchi have all made a special study of gunfit. Having noted earlier that Beretta have recently reintroduced the off-set comb stock, I will say no more here about that firm other than I have found their products very well engineered and durable: they win competitions. Perazzi, although a much newer, and smaller, company, also has an enviable record of competition success. Like Beretta, they have combined the skills of craftsmen with the latest engineering technology. Their gunfitting procedure is particularly interesting. They can now fit a customer for a gun in the traditional way, punch the customer's measurements into a computer-driven cutting machine, and produce, in minutes, a partially completed stock which can be ready for test firing an hour or two later. Franchi's special contribution to gunstock design is their radically different *Calcio Ergonomico* (ergonomically shaped stock). To quote their latest advertising literature: 'This innovation has been developed to permit recoil to discharge itself in a perfectly straight line, in so doing eliminating any perceivable muzzle flip and therefore permitting the second shot to be discharged in the same line of fire.' I have not yet had the chance to shoot the new stock, but it is clearly designed for trap shooters rather than the sporting, skeet or game fraternity. The idea upon which the design is based – recoil is more controllable when directed in a straight line – is perfectly sound. One suspects that muzzle flip, if not eliminated, will be significantly reduced by the design.

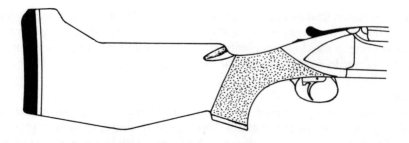

Franchi's *Calcio Ergonomico*, the idea of which is to keep the force of recoil in a straight line and therefore keep muzzle flip and discomfort to a minimum.

However, trial by the ordeal of competition is the only way to see if a new idea like this really offers a significant advantage.

All praise to Beretta, Perazzi and Franchi, they are an indication of what might have happened to the British gun trade but did not. However, I will end this chapter on a cautionary note. Considered in the world-wide context, modern production methods have, I believe, had an adverse effect on gun design and fit. Some of the subtleties of the past in such things as grip and comb and butt sole shape seem recently to have become lost as guns are turned out by a work force of robots and cost accountants. More positively, it is probable that a scientific consideration of ergonomics will soon be more generally applied to shotgun design.

## NOTES

1 I can also confirm Greener's latter comment about guns in Australia; in a trip to that country in 1990, I was able to examine a large number of old English guns made for the colonial market – nearly all had more drop than one might have expected on a contemporary gun for the home market.

2 There are some signs that this is beginning to change. Americans have been influenced by a steady trickle of English guns and gunfitters arriving on their shores, and also, in recent years especially, by very large quantities of guns made by firms like Browning and Beretta being imported with cast. American shooters are more aware of cast than they were, but most still buy mass-produced, relatively cheap, cast-less guns made by companies like Mossberg and Remington.

# PART TWO

# The Theory and Mechanics of Gunfit

# 4

## THE BASIC VARIABLES OF GUNFIT

We have considered in some detail the history of gunfit and gun stock design, now it is time to consider the practical subject of gunfitting and we must start by defining and considering some of the basic variables of gunfit. The fundamental variables of gunfit are **length, pitch, cast** and **drop** (also known as bend).

### Length
The length of a gun stock (also called 'length of pull' or just 'pull') is the distance from the centre of the trigger (front trigger with double trigger guns) to the middle of the butt sole (or the point where the distance from trigger to butt sole is shortest). A professional gun-fitter will also measure the length from the centre of the trigger to the heel or bump of the butt and from the centre of the trigger to the toe of the butt, this effects the *pitch* which we will consider shortly. It is important to understand the difference between heel and bump: heel should mean the point at the very top of the butt sole, bump may be used to describe the protrusion that is visible on many butt soles just below the heel. Some modern guns do not have much, if any protrusion, nevertheless it is a definite aid to positive butt location. Similarly, the longest point of the stock is not always the measurement from the centre of the trigger to the toe, some guns have another bump just above the toe; to distinguish between the two I suggest the terms 'heel bump' and 'toe bump'.

The vast majority of guns measure in the range of 12½ in. to 16½ in. (length to centre) with ninety per cent of men being accommodated in the range 14 to 15½ in. The basic rule with length is that *the shooter should have as long a gun stock as he can comfortably and consistently mount and swing*. A gun with a long stock points better than a gun with a short stock and, providing it is not too long, controls recoil better. An excessively long stock will be difficult to mount and swing without checking. It may also cause the butt sole to be placed either on the arm, or low – causing the gun to shoot to one side and/or high. Conversely, too short a stock tends to be held in less than firm contact with the shoulder. Why? Because a short stock can reduce the angle between the upper and lower arm to the point where tension is created[1] –

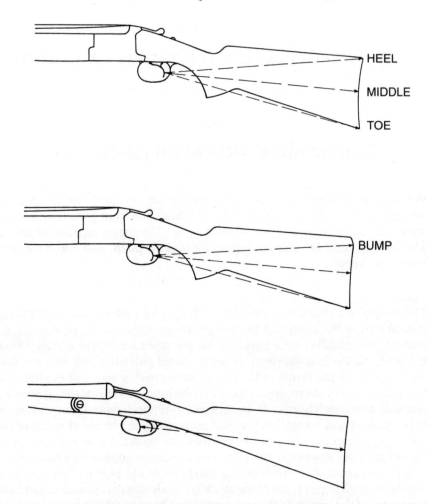

Measuring for length. Note with double trigger gun (bottom diagram), one measures length from front trigger.

the natural remedy for this is to hold the gun out a little. A gun held without full shoulder support will produce a sudden jolt rather than a progressive push when fired, causing the hands to take much more of the recoil than they might otherwise. (They should always absorb some: experienced shots use them in this shock absorbing way far more efficiently than beginners.) Like too long a stock, too short a stock may check the swing and in the case especially of light double-triggered guns is a frequent cause of bruised second fingers on the trigger hand.

Correct stock length can only be precisely ascertained by shooting targets. In the preliminary stages of assessing the correct length, the fitter will nevertheless take note of the client's arm length, muscularity (many well-built men seem to prefer shorter stocks) and mounting style. The popular test for length, which involves holding the gun at the grip and seeing if the rear of the butt makes contact with the crook of the arm/lower part of the biceps when the arm is bent at 90 degrees, is a quick imprecise guide to stock length but nothing else. Much the same may be said for the other popular technique for checking length: the 'nose and finger' method. With this, the gun butt is adjudged to be approximately the right length if a gap of two or, sometimes, three fingers widths (1½ or about 2¼ in.[2]) is visible between the nose of the shooter and the base of thumb of the hand on the grip. The nose and finger method – which, again, has its uses if its limitations are recognised – goes wrong most notably when incorrect head placement on the comb gives a false impression of the stock length requirement.

When judging the suitable length, fitters should also be careful that the client is not compensating for a too long or short a stock by altering the position of his or her forward hand. It is well known that one may compensate for a short stock by bringing the front hand forward, and for a long one by bringing the front hand back towards the action. Although one might argue the point,[3] I believe most people shoot best with the front hand positioned about midway on the forend. It may therefore be necessary to slightly alter a shooter's technique in this respect to achieve the best possible fit for length. We might add here that the line between the shooting instructor and the gunfitter can never be clearly drawn; most fitting sessions will have some sort of instructional/advice element as well.

Another point concerning fitting for length is thickness of clothing. It is a basic principle of all gunfitting that a client should be fitted for a gun in the clothing in which he or she intends to shoot; this is an especially important consideration in respect of length. Shooters may even need different guns for different times of year. Taking an extreme case, someone shooting sporting clays in a thin vest in the summer will not be happy with the same gun, if it is correctly fitted to them in respect of length, wearing thermals and a parka wildfowling in January. My own game gun is deliberately ¼ in. shorter than the one I use for sporting clays to accommodate thicker winter clothes. The alternative gun route is not the only possible remedy. Guns with interchangeable stocks like the Perazzi offer another solution, as do the new interchangeable recoil pads (which are available in various lengths). Perhaps the simplest solution is a spacer positioned behind a butt plate or recoil pad which can be removed in the Spring. A less than perfect solution is provided by the traditional rubber or leather butt extender.

## Pitch

Length, we have noted, is measured to centre, to bump/heel and to toe. The length to bump/heel and the length to toe will effect the *pitch* or 'stand' of the gun. Pitch concerns the angle of the stock 'sole' – the rear surface of the gun

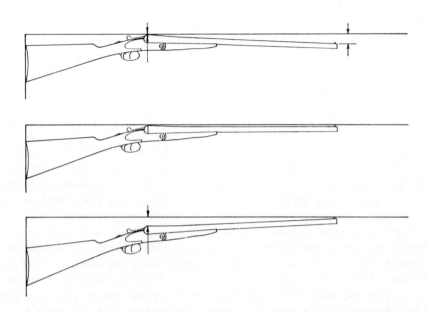

Pitch measured by distance at the muzzles from the perpendicular.

butt – relative to the axis of the bore. It is easily (but imprecisely) measured by placing the butt on the floor next to a vertical post or wall. With the top of the breech touching the post or wall, it is a simple procedure to measure any variation of the barrels at the muzzle from the perpendicular.

However, measuring pitch by distance of the muzzles from the perpendicular has disadvantages. It is significantly affected by barrel length. The measurement of pitch may be carried out much more accurately in a purpose-built jig which measures pitch in degrees rather than inches or other units of distance. For those who cannot afford, or have not the time to make a jig, pitch in degrees may also be measured by using a short and long straight edge and a simple protractor. The long straight edge is placed on the gun's rib so that it extends back just beyond the heel of the butt, the short straight edge is held against the butt sole, the protractor is then used to read the angle of pitch).

Pitch is usually downwards. With a gun set up for game shooting or sporting clays, an average pitch down measurement for a side-by-side would be about 4 degrees or 2 in. (measured in the latter case from the perpendicular surface to the top surface of the barrel or rib) and a little more, 5 - 6 degrees or $2^1/_2$ - 3 in. for an over-and-under; less pitch than this may, practically speaking, make a gun shoot high, because pitch effects the way the gun is mounted. In his pioneering work *The Shotgun Stock*, Robert Arthur, who is fully aware of the merits of measuring pitch in degrees, quotes the imperial measurements recommended or used by some of the great authorities, most of them are taken from sources written in the heyday of the side-by-side: 'Askins, 1¼ – 2¼ in. down; Churchill 2 in. down: Greener [W.W], neutral; Keith [Elmer Keith, the American gun writer], 1 – 2 in. down; Nichols [Bob Nichols another American writer] 1 – 2 in. down; O'Connor [Jack O'Connor a famous American expert], 1 – 1½ in. down (26 in. barrels); and Sell 2 in. down [yet another US author]'.

It should be noted that the point of impact of a sporting shotgun *which is used from the 'gun down' position* may be significantly altered by pitch variation. It is certainly a more important factor in gun-fit than generally realised. Traditionally, English gunfitters were much concerned with pitch, Arthur Hearn notes that in some cases a prominent toe, and hence reduced pitch, was required to keep one's elevation correct on a target. I have also observed a tendency to shoot below high quartering or crossing targets, which may, arguably, be reduced by decreasing down pitch, and hence creating a gun stock which stays up on line more easily. On the other hand, pronounced toes can cause discomfort. Some men with well-developed pectoral muscles and most women will benefit from a gun set up with a reduced toe measurement and hence more down pitch. Generally (a word that needs to be used a great deal in this book), I find that many mass-produced over-and-under guns have toes which are too prominent and/or too sharp for the average user.

Pitch effects the way the gun beds into the shoulder. A gun in which the pitch and butt contour is not set up correctly will reduce flesh contact at the butt sole causing the recoil of the gun to be applied to a smaller area of the shoulder than might otherwise be the case. It is more debatable whether or not pitch will effect point of impact significantly in a gun which is used in the trap style, pre-mounted. I retain an open mind, it seems conceivable that it could, not least because pitch will effect the way the gun meets the shoulder and therefore the way it rotates at the shoulder in recoil. However, I would also note that one extremely experienced gunfitter (Alan Rhone) has told me that he is convinced after a series of experiments that this is not the case in trap guns. Alan accepts, however, that pitch will alter the way the stock is brought to the shoulder and hence may, practically, effect shot placement in guns used from the gun-down position. He noted on an early manuscript of this book 'In the case of an aimed [trap] gun, with middle and front beads held in a figure of eight, I cannot find any change in point of impact caused by changes of pitch. However, toe prominence may cause the gun to 'come up short' and hence cause it to shoot high, with down pitch having the opposite effect. Pitch changes probably have a greater effect on sporting guns than trap guns'.

What we are trying to achieve in a well-fitted gun is a butt sole which comes up to shoulder naturally and which maximises flesh contact throughout its length. I do not like to see the toe or the heel of the butt coming to the shoulder first. Over-and-unders generally want a little more pitch down than side-by-sides, as noted, and it certainly seems the case that the average mass-produced over-and-under made in the 1980s or 1990s has more down pitch than side-by-sides typically have. Whether or not this is related to the tendency of over-and-unders to shoot higher than side-by-sides and the manufacturer's belief that pitch variation is part of the answer would be to return to the debate left open in the previous paragraph. All gunfitters should be aware that guns do move both in the vertical and horizontal planes during recoil and that there is more movement than the muzzle flip and rearwards acceleration which is easily visible. My own observation is that all other things being equal, over-and-unders are prone to high shooting (especially as far as the top barrel is concerned – its point of inertia at the shoulder is higher causing more rotation in the second phase of recoil) and side-by-sides to low shooting (which is probably explained by actual flexing of the barrels and of the grip when the gun is fired). It is notable that the shooting literature of the pre–1970 period, the era when the side-by-side was king in Great Britain, is full of references to low shooting guns and means of curing the deficiency; it is much rarer to see this condition discussed in the age of the over-and-under. Shooting instructors and fitters should also bear in mind that the trajectory of clay targets is very different to live birds: clays drop.

If a gun is fitted with a recoil pad or butt plate, temporary adjustments to pitch may be made by loosening off the fixing screws and inserting some sort of packing – cardboard strips, washers, coins – between the rear of the stock and the pad or plate. In guns fitted with recoil pads, it is also possible to change pitch or contour of the butt sole by grinding the rear surface of the pad.

### Length and pitch – other considerations
As well as the length to centre, heel/bump and toe, length may sometimes be measured to either side of the sole of the butt. As already noted, many older guns (at least the ones which have survived in their original state) will have subtly-shaped butt soles. W.W. Greener notes: '[a gun stock] in most cases should be slightly shorter to the left edge of the butt-plate than to the right [for a right-hander]'. Although I have found no practical advantage to this, I think the comments of so knowledgeable a man as W.W. Greener are, nevertheless, worth taking seriously.

The great Birmingham gunmaker also records that the famous exhibition shooter, Doctor W.F. Carver always insisted on a gun 'with a heel-plate, not only much hollowed – i.e., very much shorter to the centre than to the extremities – but also chamfered [bevelled] so as to fit squarely against the muscles of his shoulder'. Greener's rationale, which I fully endorse, was simple: 'The better and more truly the butt fits the shoulder the more comfortable will be the gun in use, and the less appreciable will be the recoil'.

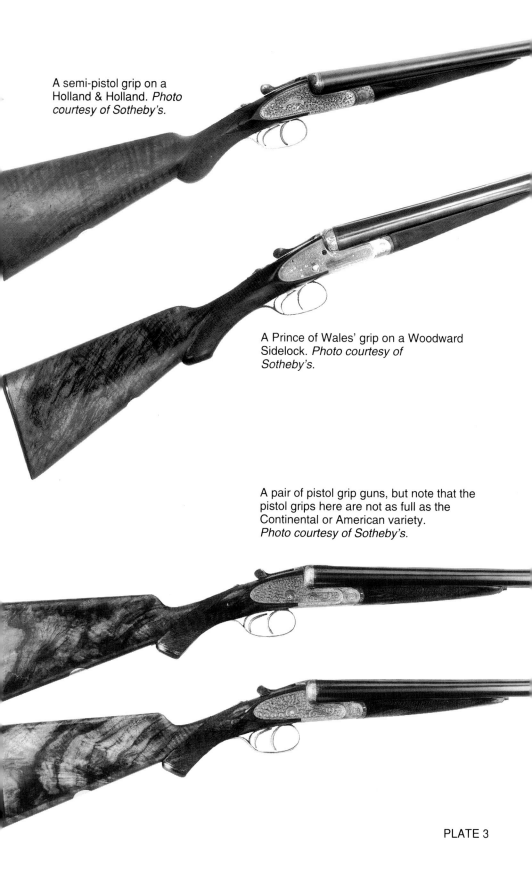

A semi-pistol grip on a Holland & Holland. *Photo courtesy of Sotheby's.*

A Prince of Wales' grip on a Woodward Sidelock. *Photo courtesy of Sotheby's.*

A pair of pistol grip guns, but note that the pistol grips here are not as full as the Continental or American variety. *Photo courtesy of Sotheby's.*

PLATE 3

A pair of Rigby guns. The stocks are interesting because they show very clearly how the length to bump can be significantly different from length to heel.

Two Italian guns by Zoli. The upper one is an over-and-under sporter with a pistol grip and schnabel forend. The bottom gun is a side-by-side 20-bore with a copy of an English stock, although it is slightly unusual in that the straight grip has been combined with a single trigger.

A modern over-and-under game gun by Ruger, again combining a straight grip with a single trigger. The advantages of this are debatable, in that the straight-gripped stock is most commonly seen on double trigger guns when the feature facilitates the movement of the trigger finger and gripping hand.

PLATE 4

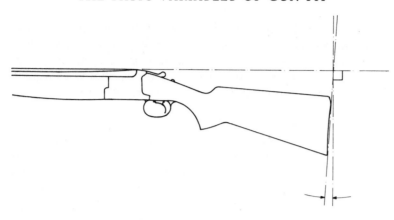

Measuring pitch by angle.

Clearly, W.W. thought the shape of butt sole especially important; he recommended 'a large butt, not too flat, with a fairly broad toe'. The modern trend, led by Robert Churchill, is for flatter butts, but there is still great variation between guns. I would make two comments. First, someone who shoots with the gun on, or partially on, the shoulder joint rather than in the so-called shoulder pocket may require a more concave butt sole, second I note the opinion of Andrew Perkins of Holland & Holland: 'I believe that the ideal butt sole should be concave – to whatever degree best suits the in-dividual – and will include bumps high and low on the butt sole. These provide a precise index of location. Without them it is more difficult for the shooter to be aware of small errors in mounting.'

One might state a general rule that *the shape of butt sole should match the user and be as wide and as long as may be consistently mounted.* This dictum should need little explanation: the greater the surface area of the butt sole (assum-ing good contact with the shoulder), the greater the area through which recoil is transmitted, and hence the more comfortable the gun will feel in recoil. It is also worth emphasising that many shooters use guns which are shaped so as to be in only partial contact with the shoulder.

Butt sole length and width are rarely mentioned in shooting literature, even though it is clear that human beings do not come in the standard sizes mass producers of firearms would prefer. From a gunfitting point of view there will be some trial and error involved when fitting for these variables. In most cases the top of the butt sole should position in line with or very slightly below the top of the shoulder and extend down to the bottom edge of the pectoral muscle. The vast majority of modern sporting shotguns fall in the range of 1⅝ to 2 in. for width at the middle of the butt sole, and 4⅞ to 5⅝ in. for the depth from heel to toe. Typical measurements on an over-and-under would be 1¾ and 5⅛ in. Some modern guns with long stocks, or extended stocks have excessively long butt soles because the stocker has merely added length without adequately considering the proportions of the finished butt sole. If as a fitter you are requesting an increase of length adding an inch or more to the stock length you should as a matter of routine specify a finished length of butt sole.

### Cast

The cast of a gun is the amount the stock is set over to the right or left in relation to the top rib/barrel line. It is measured at the comb, heel and toe. Professional gun fitters may also measure cast 'at face' (about midway between the front of the comb and the rear/heel) and 'at comb' (meaning the front of the comb). Sometimes cast starts at the rear of the top strap, and sometimes (in best guns with much cast) at the root of the action. Robert Arthur observes that on a traditionally stocked gun with a tapered comb, cast has the effect of bringing the side of the comb more or less into parallel with the line of sight. I think this is a useful insight.

A stock angled to the right is referred to as having 'cast-off' and a stock angled to the left is referred to as having 'cast-on.' The basic principle with cast is to create a gun which, when mounted, will – without significant canting of the head – allow *the shooter's master eye to be in line with the rib*. According to the British system, right-handers (with right master eyes) will usually want some cast-off and left-handers (with left master eyes) some cast-on. Broad shouldered and/or wide faced people (especially those wide faced people with narrow set eyes) will want more cast than others.[4]

Cast not only affects the eye/rib/barrel relationship in the horizontal plane, but it will also effect the horizontal placement of the butt at the shoulder. It is often stated that the butt should fit in the hollow between the collar bone and the shoulder joint known as the 'shoulder pocket'; this area, covered by the pectoral muscle and to its upper, outer, edge by the deltoid muscle, is easily identified by folding one's arms in front of the chest and then moving one of the hands up to feel for the pocket positioned immediately above (a variation on this fold-the-arms theme may also be used as an aid to placing a gun stock on a beginner's shoulder). The fact that this shoulder pocket hollow

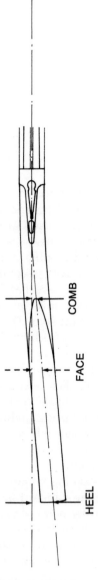

Cast: overhead view of gun cast from rear of action tang.

does not run vertically is often cited as the reason for differential cast measurements at heel and toe. I retain an open mind. Although, classically, the stock should fit snugly into the shoulder pocket hollow and the cast (and drop) adjusted accordingly, some shooters – especially those with narrow shoulders who stand edge on or obliquely to the target – will feel more comfortable with a stock which rests slightly further out, on, or partially on, the main mass of the shoulder joint (this group will not usually need much or any cast at heel and toe to achieve a comfortable fit). What may be considered absolutely wrong is to have a gun which, either because of poor gun fit or poor technique, rests on the arm/biceps. The fitter must take into account both the individual's physique and technique and decide what is most suitable, the golden rule being that anything which unnecessarily creates tension or discomfort must be wrong and should be altered if possible. Sometimes there will have to be a bit of trade-off between what the fitter would like to see and what the client feels happy with.

As far as the great majority of shooters are concerned cast is the least important of the basic variables. Many can manage surprisingly well with guns which are wrongly cast or castless. Intriguingly, some right-handed right master-eyed shooters actually appear to shoot better with cast-on guns. There are various possible explanations for these phenomena: some have adapted to a wrongly cast gun; 'wrong' cast may compensate for poor regulation or, more commonly, eccentric technique; in some cases the wrong cast may be an advantage because it prevents the shooter twisting his or her head on the stock – an aspect of cast which has not been adequately explored.

There is certainly little doubt that many experienced shooters are able to make an instantaneous or almost instantaneous correction to their head position to compensate for inappropriate cast measurements. Moreover, the shot column itself gives a certain leeway for lateral aiming error, at least as far as crossing shots are concerned, and especially those which favour the cast of the gun.[5] The experienced gunfitter will know when it is sensible to intervene to correct quirks of style which might affect cast or any other variable; sometimes, especially with people who are good performers set in their style, one will be best advised to work around a less than perfect style.

Americans probably wonder about our concern with cast: most of them have managed without it for years. The famous American gun writer, Elmer Keith positively disliked it on the grounds that it prevented firm cheeking of the gun. Would he have made the same comment had he been brought up in this country? Probably not. Whoever is right, we should all recognise how influenced we are by our experience and national traditions, and how easy it is to create dogmas which have more to do with prejudice than scientific observation.

We have seen that cast may be measured at comb, face, heel and toe. Nevertheless, many amateurs will measure cast at heel alone. This can be

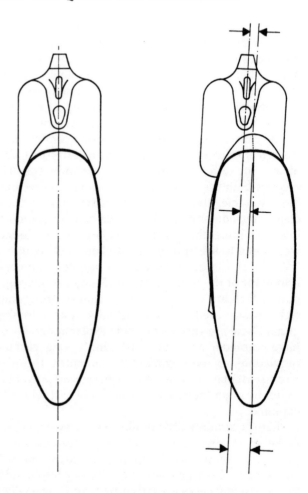

Cast: rear view of
castless gun, and
cast gun.

misleading, many combs are offset to a greater or lesser extent. Moreover, many recently made Continental and Japanese guns with very thick combs may show some cast at heel but, due to the thickness of their comb at face, will effectively have no cast off at face at all (indeed some Continental guns showing cast-off at heel are actually cast-on at face). Not measuring cast at toe is also potentially misleading because so many guns have different measurements for cast at heel and toe, whether or not it was the manufacturer's intention that they should.

People with broad, full chests and women may benefit from a little extra cast at toe (and a toe which is not pointed): $3/16$ in. at heel and $5/16$ or $3/8$ in. at toe would be very typical, traditional cast measurements. Many fitters would say that this remains a good average for a side-by-side, although I would risk stating that an over-and-under will probably, on average, want less. Why?

Partly it is subjective, an excessively cast over-and-under feels wrong to me, somehow it does not seem to match the single sighting plane of these guns, but there is also a more scientific reason. Gough Thomas demonstrated that cast (at heel) in one direction can cause a gun to shoot in the other, particularly one with superposed barrels. The essential problem as Thomas, a trained engineer, observed is that 'the thrust of recoil and the reaction to it offered by the shooter's shoulder do not take place along the same line' in the cast gun. If one imagines a gun with an extreme of cast, the point should be clear. The more the stock is bent in one direction the more the barrels are out of line with the butt sole, and the more the recoil will cause the gun to move to the opposite direction when it is fired *in spite of the fact that rib and eye may be in alignment in the horizontal plane.*

However, this is less of a problem in side-by-sides because the right barrel, the most used barrel, is in line, roughly, with the heel, and hence when it is fired the recoil is directed more or less in a straight line. Should we all return to side-by-sides? No (although Gough Thomas would probably have supported the proposition). The left-hand barrel on a typically cast side-by-side is not in line with the heel, so it may also shoot to the left. More importantly, side-by-sides are also prone to down flip, because they are relatively thin in the grip and barrels, and prone to flexing in the vertical plane. The upshot, excuse the pun, of all this is that the gunfitter should be aware that guns and their users are not static objects. In the specific case of the over-and-under the fitter may have to consider thinning or offsetting the comb of an over-and-under as an alternative, or partial alternative, to undesirable extremes of cast.

Adjustments for cast can be made to existing stocks by heating and bending (although there is always some risk of breakage involved in such procedures), or by removing wood at the head of the stock. I always prefer to have guns adjusted at the head – although it is not always that popular with stockers – because as well as eliminating any risk of breakage, one knows that the stock will stay in position even if subjected to baking sunlight.[6]

Cast is usually applied so that the comb is angled relative to the line of the rib. As a comb significantly angled to the axis of the rib will increase felt recoil, we may state *the less cast the better*, especially at heel.

An oddity about cast worth noting and which concerns some older guns, and a few modern guns which have been altered by old school craftsmen, is that one may discover they have been 'scooped' at face (or indeed may have been made with a 'swept face'). 'Scooping' means that wood has been removed from the stock at the point of facial contact to help bring the eye in line with the rib (a swept face gun is similar in principle but the sweep is blended into the stock with a longer, smoother, concave curve); such guns may show a little cast at heel, but, effectively, they will have considerably more at the face where it really counts. A fitter should always remember that he has the option of scooping, thinning or offsetting the comb as well as

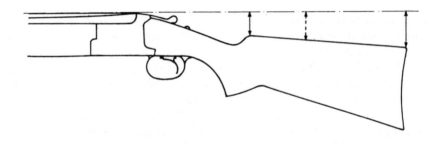

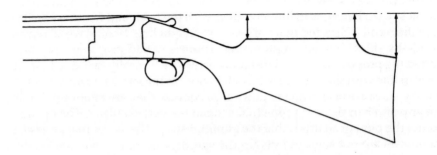

Measuring for drop. *(above)* Drop at comb, face and heel on conventional stock. *(below)* Drop at comb, monte and heel, on Monte Carlo stock.

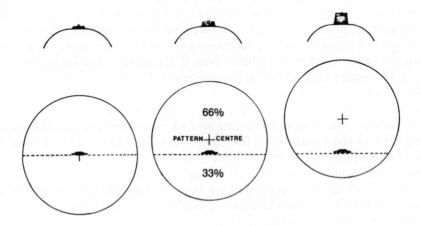

All sorts of opinions have been expressed as to the right pattern placements for various shotgun sports. In truth, what is right is what suits the individual; there is no simple formula.

bending the stock to achieve the right eye-to-rib alignment. Another way to manipulate cast at heel and toe is to offset the recoil pad slightly, or fit a purpose-built adjustable pad. I would, normally, only recommend the latter as a sensible option on trap guns; adjustable pads are not really conducive to quick, glitch-free mounting in skeet and sporting shooting. They can also alter the balance of a gun significantly. The best adjustable pad available (and one of the lightest), is the 'Jones Adjuster' which may be obtained from and fitted by Alan Rhone of 37 Cae Gabriel, Penycae, Wrexham, Clwyd, who is also well known for his excellent adjustable comb conversions.

## Drop

Drop (or bend), arguably the most crucial measurement of all, is the amount the top edge of the stock is set down relative to the top of the sighting rib (a gun must have some drop or the muzzle of the gun would always come up above the point of aim). Drop has two functions; the most important is to locate the shooting eye just above the breech, so that the view to target is unobstructed and the relationship between the barrels and the target may be easily established.

Drop is usually measured 'at comb' and 'at heel', but it may also be usefully measured at the point of facial contact on the stock comb. As well as establishing the eye rib relationship in the vertical plane, drop, like cast, is also a prime factor in locating the sole of the butt at the shoulder. It should be adjusted/adjudged before drop at comb or face for this reason: correct placement at the shoulder creates the datum by which drop at comb and face can be calculated.

For most people the gun stock should fit at heel so that the top of the heel is in line with or *very slightly* below the top of the shoulder, though some prefer to mount their guns lower (for example many Italian trap shooters as noted earlier, not to mention the great British sporting shot, Barry Simpson). Fit for drop at face and heel is affected both by physique and shooting style. Get into the habit of looking at facial features. Analyse style carefully. Some people raise their shoulder more than others during the gun mount, this is particularly true of those with longish necks who shoot in the classic tradition where the gun is pushed towards the line of the bird and the shoulder brought up to meet it. The requirement for drop at heel will obviously be affected by such individual differences.

Classically, the drop should be adjusted *so that the gun will pattern about two thirds above the point of aim* (for trap shooting arguably higher, for sporting clays and skeet, arguably a bit lower – my preference for sporting is a 60:40 pattern or even a little flatter – the variable being that many sporting targets are missed over the top.) A gun which shoots a fraction high is potentially advantageous to most users not just because it gives a little built-in lead to rising or driven targets, but because on the majority of shots, it allows one to keep the target in view. Some individuals will prefer to see a larger gap than others and hence will want a higher shooting gun. No absolute rule can be made here, although we may say that few shots would be well served with a gun which shot below the mark. I also note than those who are deliberate aimers may require more drop than those who keep their eyes glued to the target and nothing but the target. Conscious aimers (and I do not advocate the practice) tend to bring the foresight up so that it touches the bottom of the bird. Those who rely on visual contact with the target alone seem to see a greater gap. John Brindle makes the useful distinction between 'brushers' and 'blotters'. Brushers position the moving gun under the line of the bird, blotters come right up on the line and may even go above the line. Obviously each has very different gunfitting requirements.

To ascertain if the drop (and cast) is *approximately* correct, the fitter looks down the muzzels towards the shooter (but *never* attempt this unless both fitter and shooter have proven the gun empty to each other's satisfaction). In the case of the classic $1/3 - 2/3$ fit, the iris (the coloured part) of the shooter's eye should, ideally, appear to be sitting on the rib/breech with the top of the rib just cutting into the bottom edge of the iris and with the butt level with, or just below, the top of the shoulder. As with all other checks by eye, this one is at best approximate: only the pattern plates and targets will give definitive answers. The technique of individual shooters vary and the regulation of guns vary: it is never possible to fit a gun without seeing the gun and firer in action as a whole. Nevertheless, I will put in print, that with a well regulated gun and with head properly located on stock, the shooter should be able to see at least $1/8$ in. of rib (i.e., the eye will be positioned at least $1/8$ in. above the top surface of the rib). Moreover, and it will be affected both by the pitch of the rib relative to the bore and by the drop and pitch of the stock, his or her eye should not be aware of a rib which is falling away or obviously climbing. I emphasise, however, the figure of $1/8$ in. is only a guide: some shooters will prefer to see significantly more.

Bearing in mind my previous comments on regulation, it is interesting to note the comments of Mark Course, an exceptionally skilled stocker, who works for Gunmark (the United Kingdom distributor of Beretta guns and who has visited the Beretta factory in Italy). His fellow craftsmen in the Gardonne told him that in trap guns they like to see the iris sitting on the rib, and in guns designed for sporting clays, the pupil sitting on the rib as viewed from the muzzle.

The importance of drop, and especially the drop at the point of facial contact cannot be over emphasised. This is a crucial measurement, because it is the primary determinant of the eye's vertical relationship to the barrels and target. Shooters can adapt fairly easily to a gun which is too short or too long, or one which is wrongly cast. But making do with the wrong drop is far more difficult. Very slight variations ($1/16$ in. or less) are important, especially as far as the dimension at face is concerned. The shotgun user does not have the benefit of a rear sight to ensure the alignment of the barrels with the target. Instead, the eye fulfils the role of backsight, and the consistent place-

(*above*) This young man is struggling with a stock which is far too long for him.

PLATE 5

(*left*) This Beretta semi-automatic has been well mounted by an experienced shot. The fit for drop, however, looks as if it might be modified. The eye appears to be looking at the back of the action.

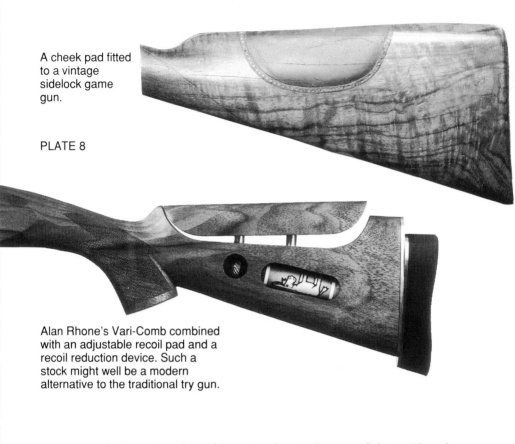

A cheek pad fitted to a vintage sidelock game gun.

PLATE 8

Alan Rhone's Vari-Comb combined with an adjustable recoil pad and a recoil reduction device. Such a stock might well be a modern alternative to the traditional try gun.

At the pattern plates. My own preference is to start fitting at 16 yards and move back.

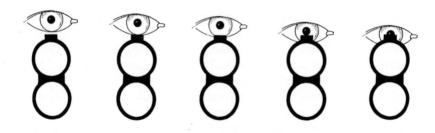

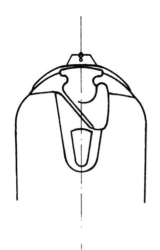

(above) These drawings represent various schools of thought on how the eye should sit above the breech. My own starting point for sporting shooting falls somewhere between the middle drawing and the one to its immediate right, but only the pattern plates and watching the client shoot at real targets will give reliable answers. The regulation of the gun, the type of gun and the individual's shooting style will all affect pattern placement.

(left) The figure eight relationship is often thought to be ideal on a twin-beaded trap gun. Much depends, however, on barrel and rib regulation.

(below) Line of sight: the eye must be placed slightly above the breech. How much will depend on individual preference for rib picture, but ¼ in. will suit many. Looking flat along the rib is a distinct disadvantage.

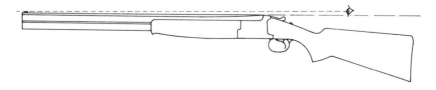

ment of the eye in relation to the bead, rib or bore axis (all functionally the same thing) is absolutely crucial. This is why drop should *routinely* be measured at the point of facial contact.

The drop at the point of facial contact is, without question, critical, but the drop at heel/shoulder is also important as already noted, and will usually be determined before drop at comb or face as noted earlier. It can fall anywhere between $1^1/_4$ and $3^1/_2$ in., with most guns measuring up between 2 and $2^1/_2$ in. People with sloping shoulders will – unless they raise their shoulder in mounting significantly – require more drop at heel than those with more level shoulders, and those with long necks may also require more (although again the requirement will be reduced if they have learnt to raise the shoulder as the gun is mounted).

If those with sloping shoulders or long necks use guns which do not have sufficient drop at heel they will naturally tend to mount the heel of the butt above the line of the shoulder. An upright stance, as favoured by British shots in the last century and many Americans to this day, will also create a need for more drop at heel than a centre-of-gravity-forward stance: as the body frame becomes more upright the distance between the cheekbone and the shoulder pocket increases.

The existence of such individual differences in physique and style which are mentioned throughout this book show up the importance to the fitter both of his knowledge of various styles and of the need to watch someone shoot in order to reliably fit them. My own rule of thumb is that, all other considerations being satisfied, *the less drop the better*. I think a crooked gun handles less naturally than a straighter one (and certainly recoils more). However, I also agree with Robert Churchill that a gun, even a high combed one, requires considerable fall in the hand/grip/wrist to handle well. A straight gun does not necessarily have to be equipped with a high, awkwardly angled, grip.

## Combs

The consideration of drop brings us naturally on to the subject of combs. The location of the eye, and its ability to return to the same location each time the gun is mounted is, as we have noted governed by the contact between the shooter's cheek and the comb of the stock. The comb of the gun should rest comfortably underneath the cheekbone in the area between the cheekbone and the jaw: the stock should not be resting on the lower jaw. The cheek should be in firm contact with the comb but not squashed down upon it. Moreover, the line of the comb should be seen to flow with the line of cheekbone (which one may imagine extending to or just below the earlobe in most people).

Having considered where the comb should be positioned in relation to the cheekbone, we may now consider the relationship between comb, cheekbone and eye socket. Interestingly, individual variation in adults in the distance from the cheekbone to the centre of the eye socket is very small although there is a sex difference: the distance in women is smaller. In the majority of adult males the distance from cheek bone to centre of pupil (with the head in a natural firing position) is about 1¾ in. plus or minus ⅛ in. In women the distance is about 1½ in. plus or minus ⅛ in., consequently women often require a higher comb than men. Children, who usually have very much smaller heads with a reduced distance from eye socket to cheekbone, will, like many women, require a higher comb (which is one of the main reasons why merely cutting down a gunstock is rarely enough modification to suit an adult gun to a young shot).

We saw in the previous section that the need for differential drop at heel can vary very significantly from individual to individual to accommodate longer or shorter necks and variations in shooting styles (viz: the high shoulder/low shoulder style of mount); we have just noted the need for differential drop at the point of facial contact varies to a smaller extent. Nevertheless, fitters must be on constant look-out for clients with abnormal facial features; I have talked so much about average measurements not because I expect readers to apply them robotically, but because they help to build up an awareness of human anatomy as it relates to gunfitting.

The relationship of gun stock to cheek, eye and shoulder, cannot be considered at just one moment in time: guns move, both in recoil, and as they are mounted and swung. The apparently static relationships between user and gun change. The rearwards movement of the comb in recoil has some very practical and potentially painful consequences.

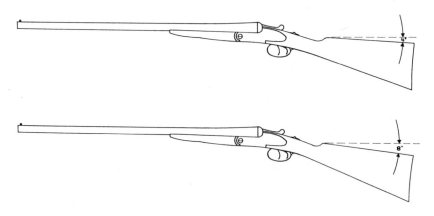

The angle of comb relative to the bore axis is a critical consideration. All other things being equal, a steeply angled comb will recoil more. The angle of the comb of a gun stock of 14½ in. with drop at comb of 1½ in. and drop at heel of 2¼ in. is about 4 degrees; I would regard this as a maximum.

Gunmakers have traditionally made guns so that the drop at comb is substantially less than the drop at heel. However, the problem with any stock which is inclined in this way is that in recoil the front part of the comb, rising in front of the cheek bone, will tend to come back and smack the shooter in the face. On the other hand a gun with a comb which is too low at face and front of the comb, or which has too much taper in the comb (or taper at the wrong place), will be difficult to mount positively because comb/cheek contact is less than ideal. Fitters should consider the fit of the comb not just in its final position, locked into the face and shoulder, but at the beginning of the final phase of mounting as well – that moment when contact between cheek and gun is first established but before there is firm contact between butt and shoulder. The general rule should be to reduce the incline of the stock to the minimum compatible with positive location.

There are several ways around the problem of excessively inclined combs:

**1:** (The most common): Keep some incline, but thin the comb of the stock ahead of the area of facial contact. This is the route taken by most of the famous London makers. Inexpertly done, tapering can lead to a loss of positive contact/location between the user's face and stock. Expertly done, it can however also be something of a miracle cure for bruised cheeks not amenable to other treatment.

**2:** (Which may be combined with 1): Shave off some or all of the slope in the stock immediately ahead of the area of facial contact (a crude method which looks a little odd when followed, but which I have also found to be a simple and effective remedy for otherwise incurable recoil blisters on the face. This is the principle of the 'hog's back' Continental stock and also W.W. Greener's 'Rational' gun stock).

**3:** Change to a stock with a 'parallel comb', i.e., one where the drop measurements are similar at comb, face and heel, or a partially parallel comb such as the Monte Carlo, which is parallel throughout most its length, only stepped down in the last inch or two to create extra drop at heel.

Quite a few skeet and sporting shots are now investigating the merits of the *parallel comb* as described above. Apart from the recoil advantage, the advocates of the parallel comb suggest mounting is more consistent because the eye/rib relationship in the vertical plane is not as seriously affected by imperfect head placement. My own opinion is that parallel combs have their place, especially for trap shooters, but the most comfortable and positively locating comb for the majority of game, sporting and skeet gun users is one which has a slight incline.

Whatever type of comb is selected, the comb is, clearly, a key part of the gun, for it establishes the vertical plane relationship between the eye and the rib. Many people with long necks and long faces or those who mount their guns very low will find that a gun with average drop dimensions will force them to cock their head down uncomfortably[7] to make contact with the comb. They may be candidates for a Monte Carlo, or a semi Monte Carlo stock. I might suggest that if fitting an individual for a traditional stock would result in a difference of comb and heel dimensions for drop of more than $7/8$ in., the Monte Carlo option should be considered very carefully.

As a general rule we might state that: *the comb should be sufficiently high for the head to fall naturally against it without any need to cock the neck down uncomfortably when the gun is mounted to the face and shoulder in the normal fashion.* Over and above the fact that too high a comb will disturb the eye/rib

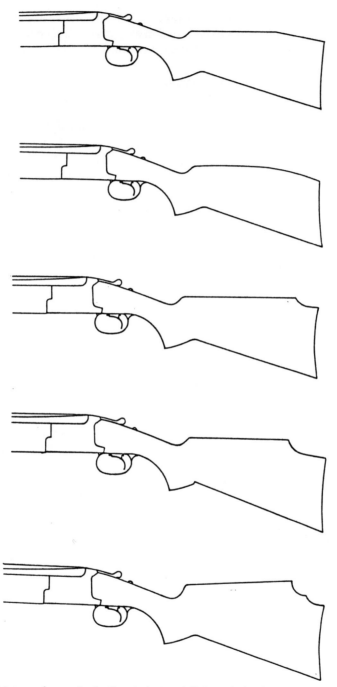

Different types of gun stock. *(top to bottom)* Robert Arthur's 'Line of sight' stock, Hogsback, semi Monte Carlo, Monte Carlo, Double Monte Carlo. All of these stocks have combs which are angled to reduce recoil.

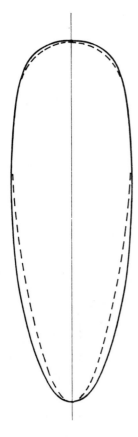

Comb width and shape is an important variable with many subtleties.

relationship, it will also cause the head to be pushed up. An excessively erect head position is unsuited to sporting shooting.

## Comb Shape

As for the shape of the comb and stock in cross section, some suggest that the narrow-faced need a bulbous, thick comb and the box headed only a narrow sliver. My own experience is not so simple. Some narrow-faced people feel more comfortable with narrow combs; some wide-faced people still prefer bulbous combs. Much depends on the distance between the eyes and the relationship of the eye socket to the cheekbone. The shape of the arch of the cheekbone must also be considered, as must the individual's technique for bringing the gun to the face. One is trying to achieve a comb which is comfortable and which locates positively and consistently. On competition guns, fine tuning may well be required in respect of comb profile – slight adjustments having quite profound effects. A squarer profile tends to locate more positively, but is not necessarily as comfortable.

My friend Andrew Perkins, an exceptional trap shot as well as a skilled gunfitter, has recently experimented with what he calls the 'compliant comb', a comb of fairly square profile made from a compliant material such as cork. Andrew also believes a comb should be fairly square in cross section to locate positively under the cheekbone and should be designed when set up for the highest performance so that the nose of the shooter touches the side of the comb thus creating a datum for consistent mounting.

Ultimately, what one is looking for is a stock which glides smoothly into the face and shoulder without any disturbance of the muzzles. Snaking of muzzles as they come up in the mount, or in the context of combs, a feeling of a glitch as the gun comes to face, may well be a sign of poor fit. All the 'gun-down' disciplines require a gun which can quickly and consistently come into the face and shoulder – this will probably be easier with a comb of medium thickness with some degree of taper. The needs for trap shooting are slightly different – one requires a gun which comes, precisely, into the same place every mount. This is often better accomplished with a thicker, more parallel and perhaps less tapered, comb. One final point regarding trapshooters: they often force or squash their cheeks down more on the comb than other shooters do. Fitters must be aware of this; it effects gunfit and the interaction of the face and butt in recoil.

## Grips

As we have seen, there is far more to gunfit than many might think. One variable, or more accurately, collection of variables which we have not yet considered is the grip size. This is another neglected but critical aspect of gunfitting. If a shooter can't grip his gun, felt recoil will be increased and muzzle control reduced.

A good grip design should not cause the hand or wrist to be uncomfortably cocked up or down. Both grip and forend should balance. I do not like to see a thin grip on the butt combined with a wide deep grip on the forend; moreover, the grip and forend should be so arranged that, as far as possible, both hands can work in the same line. Such an arrangement aids natural hand to eye co-ordination. A grip which is too high or too low relative to the forend (or vice versa) will cause the hands to operate in an uncoordinated way.

Grip dimensions are very personal but it makes sense that the size and shape of the grip should match the shooter's hand. Guns designed for clay shooting, which tend to be a bit heavier, tend also to be a bit thicker in the grip – a heavy gun with a narrow grip feels distinctly odd and vice versa). The shape of the grip must also suit the shooter's hand ergonomically. This is why in cross-section most straight grips are not circular but oval or diamond in shape; in both cases to more naturally fill the hand (a diamond shape also works well with a semi pistol grip). Grips should be deeper than they are wide. This relationship is crucial, too thick and round a grip will feel much more comfortable and no smaller if it is expertly reshaped into an ovoid or diamond shape.

The length of the grip is also an important variable in the case of semi and full pistol designs. A shooter with stubby fingers, struggling with a thick, long grip will often end up holding his gun incorrectly, as will the man with long fingers forced to use a gun with a short thin grip. This can have disastrous consequences for mounting – which is profoundly affected by the position of the right hand and arm. The grip should be made/fitted so that the area between the pad and the first joint of the trigger finger is in unstrained contact with the surface of the trigger.

A variable in gunfit at the grip which is important, but rarely considered (Robert Churchill and Peter Hawker are exceptions, see page 31), is the angle of the top and bottom straps and the consequent affect these have on the angle of the grip. It has been suggested that many English game guns are too straight in the hand. Unfortunately, one will rarely have the option to change this. When the fall in the hand is too great, however, this can sometimes be rectified by building up an oversize grip above the level of the top-strap with epoxy or similar material.

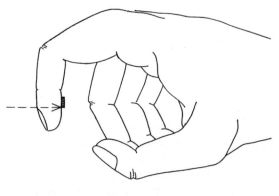

A good grip design will facilitate a natural holding position and comfortable and secure trigger finger contact with the trigger. The trigger finger should be able to pull straight back.

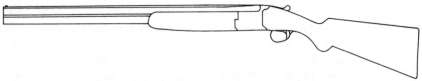

Grip and forend should be in balance. It would not make sense to put a shallow splinter forend on a side-by-side with a pronounced pistol grip. This gun looks about right.

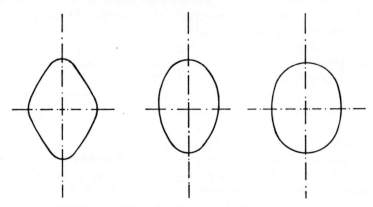

Different straight grips in cross-section.

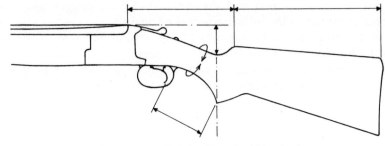

Some grip and comb dimensions; the depth and width of grip are not shown in the drawing. The relative depth and width are a most important consideration in grip design and fit.

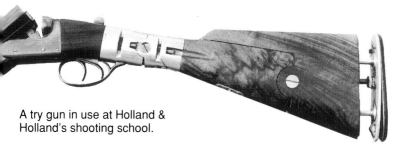

A try gun in use at Holland & Holland's shooting school.

White-washing the pattern plate before testing.

PLATE 9

This pattern distribution might be considered a little flat for some applications; my own preference for sporting clays is about 60:40, but everything depends on the individual's style.

(*above*) A paper pattern plate. Whenever erecting plates, paper or steel, one must be careful to have an adequate backstop or safety zone.

PLATE 10

Master gunfitter Andy Perkins measures a gun for length to middle.

Mass-produced, single-trigger, over-and-under guns usually have some sort of pistol grip, and, because there is no need to move onto a second trigger, they usually benefit from the increased controllability or leverage of these designs. However, some people simply do not get on with full pistol grips, in which case these may be easily converted to a semi-pistol or even straight pattern which may better suit those with a need for a longer grip.

Many old English side-by-sides with straight-hand stocks are very thin in the grip because they have been refinished a number of times. There is very little one can do about this, other than re-stock the gun. If this route is taken one should consider the Prince of Wales grip as an option. It combines the straight-hand grip's advantage (principally that one may easily move the finger back onto the second trigger) with a little more control of the muzzles.

A good stocker can usually modify the grip of a mass-produced gun to make it feel altogether different and more comfortable in the hand. As well as obvious changes in shape and size, he may remove wood from the front of the comb, and he may adjust the flutes to either side of the front of the comb. Although I like well-designed pistol grips, I think that the pistol grips on many mass-produced guns feel wrong. Robert Churchill suggested pistol grips can check the swing: I would support the proposition in so far as it applies to poorly-designed pistol grips.

I have been experimenting for several years with a slightly deepened, anatomically shaped semi-pistol which combines the natural pointing of the straight grips with the control of the pistol designs. I call it a three-quarter grip. I find it has the steadiness, and leverage of the full pistol grip with the natural pointability of the semi. It seems particularly suited to sporting clay guns, and may also be useful for one armed shooters.

Many shooters dislike the palm swells that are common on the grips of some imported guns and which can cause guns to shoot high because they force the hand to position itself too far up the stock. It is an easy matter to remove or reduced a palm swell. A custom fitted palm swell is a boon, but the crude mis-positioned lumps attached to the grips of some modern guns offer no benefits whatsoever.

A problem which afflicts many Continental imports is that the grip is too narrow at the top, but broad at the bottom. What usually happens when a grip is narrow at its top but broad below, is that the hand is pushed forward in recoil. There are two ways around the problem: either modify the grip so that its depth is relatively even throughout most of its length – the best course when the shooter uses a style which pushes the gun towards the target and brings the shoulder in behind – or go to the other extreme and create a grip which may more easily pulled back into the shoulder, like the famous Etchen type which is particular effective in controlling the muzzle flip of trap guns.

When one is making adjustments to the grip it may also be worthwhile considering a change in checkering. I prefer grip checkering which is made

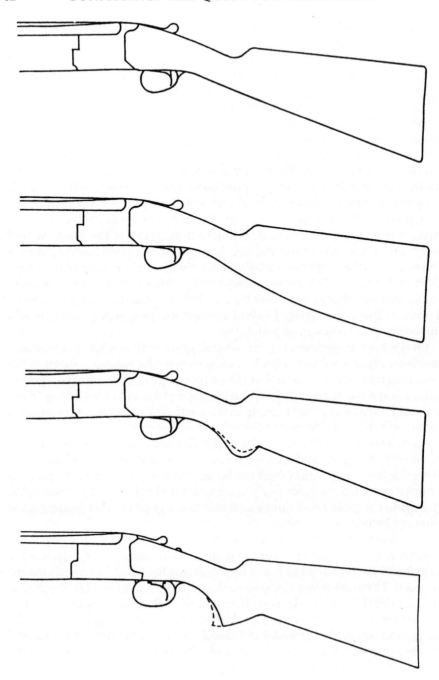

Different grip types. *(top to bottom)*: straight hand stock, swan neck stock, half pistol, full pistol. Not shown is the Prince of Wales design seen on some best quality side-by-sides *(see Plate 3)*.

up of fairly broad, but not sharp 'diamonds'. Checkering may be spaced anything between 16 and 32 lines per inch. Functionally, something in the range 20–26 works best.

I have not yet had the opportunity, but would like to experiment with synthetic rubber grips on shotguns similar to those which are fitted to pistols and revolvers: such grips help the hand to keep a secure hold of the gun and absorb some recoil.

## Triggers

The length and style of grip effects placement of the finger on the trigger. A well-shaped grip, properly held, will allow the trigger finger to be extended without twisting. It will ensure that inertia operated single-trigger mechanisms function consistently. We noted in the grip section that the trigger finger should make contact with the trigger just forward of the first joint (although some suggest it should locate on the first joint – I dislike this position because it reduces trigger control which, contrary to popular belief, is as important in shotgun marksmanship as it is in rifle or pistol shooting). The trigger should also feel comfortable to the user both as regards its angle, breadth and shape. Many mass-produced guns benefit greatly from having their triggers filed and/or bent to shape by a skilled gunmaker. I have a Winchester over-and-under modified by an ex-Purdey craftsman in this respect: the gun was transformed by this apparently minor modification.

## Trigger Pulls

Good trigger pulls are absolutely vital to good shooting: bad pulls ruin your timing (I would go as far as to say that good pulls are nearly as important as good gunfit). Trigger pulls should be adjusted to personal preference as long as they are within the safety limitations recommended by the manufacturer or gunsmith. There are, however, some general points worth noting:

1:  All trigger pulls should be adjusted to break 'cleanly' without creep.

2:  Generally, heavier guns will want (relatively) slightly heavier pulls than lighter ones.

3:  The second pull should usually be a little heavier than the first.

Boxlock guns will not adjust down as much as sidelocks, or guns like the Perazzi with sophisticated boxlock/trigger plate mechanisms using leaf springs. Typically, an 8 lb boxlock over-and-under gun should be adjusted to about 3 lb for the first pull, 3¼ lb for the second (some would say 3½ and 4, or even 4 and 4½). The best sidelocks may be adjusted even lower, however, one must take care, too light a pull can be dangerous, especially on a game gun.

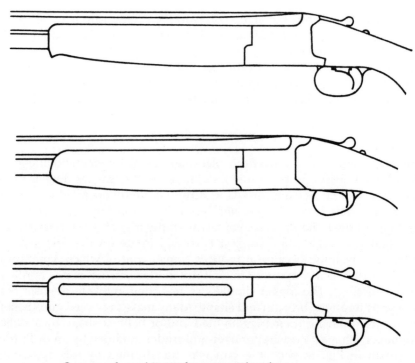

Common forend types for over-and-unders.

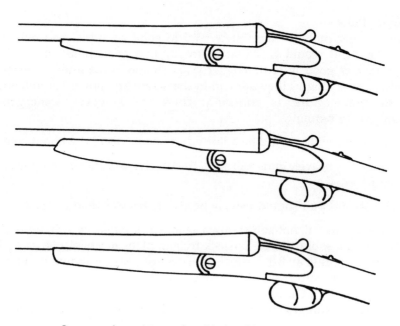

Common forend types for side-by-sides.

## Forends

Yet another subject we have not touched on so far is forends. We may identify four common types: the *splinter* (common to English side-by-side game guns), the *Schnabel* (seen on many Continental over-and-under sporters), the wide, almost flat-bottomed *beavertail* (a favourite of American side-by-sides users), and the parallel-sided fairly full *trap* forend common on over-and-unders (and not restricted to trap guns alone).

Each of these designs has its variants. In pre-war days, the extended splinter was favoured by many pheasant shooters who emulated the straight left arm style of George V. Purdey are famous for their full splinter, which has a rounded end, and which many people consider an ideal all round side-by-side design; Purdey also make a beautiful beavertail. Whilst considering the forends for side-by-sides, we might note the existence of the leather-covered spring steel handguard. This accessory, which slips over the barrels but leaves the view of the rib unobstructed, protects the hand from heat and also acts as an extension of the splinter forend.

As far as the stacked barrel guns are concerned, there is the tulip variant of the Schnabel, which swells in its middle. This allows for positive location in the hand. The beaver tail is sometimes made in extended form as the splinter used to be, and an extended design is also common to the parallel-sided over-and-under Trap-type forend. The latter, when not excessively thick, is very controllable and, though it adds some weight to the gun, is my favourite for sporting use. As an additional feature it may have some sort of finger grooves, which if well positioned are a useful aid to positive and consistent location of the forward hand.

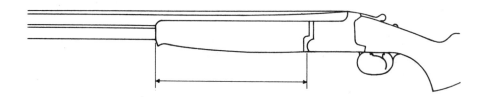

The length of the forend should be measured from the knuckle of the action.

Any forend (with the exception of the splinter) should be long enough for the shooter to grip comfortably; excessive length beyond that merely adds weight. Whatever the specifics – which are largely a matter of personal preference – a good forend design should accord plenty of control to the left hand, be unobtrusive, and encourage the gun to move flowingly in the hands of the shooter. As we have already discussed, the forend should also

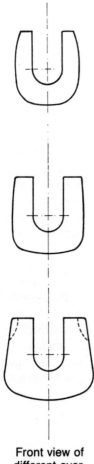

Front view of different over-and-under forends. My own preference (at least for sporting clays and game shooting) is for grips and forends which keep the hands close to the line of the barrels.

complement the grip shape and thickness. A very thin-gripped gun will feel odd with a thick forend and vice versa. If forend and grip put hands at very different heights, they are not likely to move as they should, smoothly and in concert. Too deep or wide a forend may cause the shooter to lose some of his or her natural pointing ability.[8] Finally, as with the grip, checkering on the forend is an important consideration. I prefer relatively fine checkering on a forend, if it is too coarse, as it tends to be on some guns made in Japan, it can be most uncomfortable in recoil. There is no reason why the grip and forend checkering should match other than tradition.

### NOTES

1   Assuming a gun being used off the right shoulder the angle at the crook of the elbow of the right arm is usually about ninety degrees when the gun is mounted.

2   Some American authorities suggest the gap need only be ½ in. or even less (phenomenal trap shooter Kay Ohye suggests only ⅛ in. between the face and hand), the minimum I have ever heard recommended in Great Britain is ¾ in. The old idea for trap guns was that they should be slightly longer in the stock because they were used premounted. Observing some of the best modern trap shots, however, one sees quite a few short stocks, though my own preference is for a longer stock on a trap gun because I prefer the pointing characteristics of a longer stock. I think it would be dangerous to set down any general rule.

3   George Digweed for example, the top sporting shot, favours a front hand position closer to the action.

4   My own view on cast is that it is essential for some people, but should be used with discretion, not least because it can increase felt recoil. I particularly dislike extremes of cast on over-and-unders. As far as cast at heel is concerned my normal maximum would be ¹/₂ in. on a side-by-side and ³/₈ in. on an over-and-under. Although, of course, one may increase the cast at comb to achieve the cast at face required.

5   Shot does not leave a smoothbore barrel in a spherical swarm, but in an extended column, the length of which is effected by the degree of choke. In a full choked gun the shot column at forty yards is about 11 feet long.

6   I know of one case where a competition gun being used in an international match was altered using the traditional heat and bend method. It was left in a rack in strong

sunlight, and when its owner came to pick it up, the stock had moved back to its original dimensions.

7   I have added the qualification 'uncomfortably' because most shooters tend anyway to push their neck forward and lower the chin *slightly* prior to mounting. This is not a fault in style, but a position which is a natural consequence of a determined stance. A problem only arises when tension is introduced by a strained head and neck position.

8   Forend depth can also have a subtle effect on mean point of impact. A very deep forend may cause the Mean Point of Impact (MPI) to be raised slightly, especially if the shooter is used to a pattern of forend when their hand is closer to the barrel.

# 5

## PRACTICAL FITTING

**Preliminary Considerations**
We have looked at the primary variables of gunfitting, now it is time to consider, practically, how to go about the business of gunfitting. Perhaps the first thing to state is that *before anyone can be properly fitted for a gun, they must be able to shoot*. There is absolutely no point going to the time and trouble of fitting someone for a gun if he does not have the rudimentary skills of shooting. Before any attempt is made at serious gun fitting, the shooter must be able to mount a gun with consistency and also to hit simple targets. One must, however, make a qualification – a complete beginner should start shooting with a gun reasonably appropriate to his or her physique (length is the prime consideration initially, but drop is also important[1]).

Having recognised the importance of basic competence on behalf of the client-to-be-fitted, one might note that a fundamental principle in practical gunfitting is that *one is never considering a person or gun alone, but how the combination of person and gun interact*. Therefore, it may be stated safely that *proper gunfit can only be achieved by watching someone shoot*. Some gunmakers have suggested that an individual can be adequately fitted for a gun merely by a careful analysis of his or her physique. This is not so; the self-fitting charts once supplied by firms like Webley and Scott and Greener, would produce no more than a gun which fitted approximately. Two people of identical build may handle their guns in very different ways and therefore require a gun of significantly different measurements. All of which is not, of course, to say that physique is not important. It is, but it is just the starting point for serious gunfitting.

Before being fitted for a gun, one should have firmly decided on a shooting style. This follows on from the two previous points. The style which one uses will affect gunfit. The classic Stanbury style, where the weight is kept on the left foot throughout the shooting process and where the body is oblique to the target, will require a different gun fit to the Churchill and Holland & Holland methods (where the weight transfers from one foot to the other and where the body is squarer to the target) or that rather ugly modern 'style' for shooting sporting clays where the shooter is almost, or absolutely, square to the target with his feet wide apart (or indeed the American methods where the weight tends to be more evenly distributed and the shoulder kept lower than in the British styles).

Fitted classically, the Stanbury shooter will require a longer gun with less cast (because his gun shoulder is further back relative to the head and his eye more in line with the barrels), while the Churchill, Holland & Holland, or clay shooter adopting the modern style described above, will need a shorter gun with more cast.

It also goes without saying that before an individual can operate effectively as either instructor or gunfitter, they must have a thorough understanding of the various shooting styles (towards this end I give a synopsis of Stanbury and Churchill systems below). The would-be instructor or gunfitter should also be a competent shot, able to demonstrate the various classic shooting methods left- and right-handed, and, as far as clay shooting is concerned be a reasonable performer at all three basic disciplines – Sporting, Skeet and Trap. At the moment this rarely appears to be the case. Too often fitting and instruction are based not on what the client needs, but on that which the instructor is familiar. I suggest all aspiring shooting instructors or gunfitters make a planned effort to broaden their shooting experience.

## Two Classic Methods of Shooting

*Stanbury*
The name of Percy Stanbury has become synonymous with one of this country's best known, and least gimmicky, shooting methods. It can be used with minor variations both for both game and clay shooting and has evolved from many sources, not least the shooting instructions of Charles Lancaster (*aka* H.A.A. Thorn). Here I will lay out what might be described as an evolved version of Stanbury's technique. The basics of it are that the feet should be at one o'clock (left) and three o'clock (right) to the point where the target is killed, that the weight is kept on the leading (left) foot throughout the shooting process (whatever the shot), and that the gun, having started on or very near the bird, should swing ahead of it with the requisite forward allowance being seen deliberately. (Contrary to popular opinion Stanbury did not advocate the so called 'swing-through' technique, he says the muzzles should be placed *on* the bird by the left hand at the beginning of the shooting process as the right hand is raising the butt to the face and shoulder.)

Let's consider now how we might actually shoot a simple crossing clay target:

**1:** First one must select a 'killing-point'. Based on the line and height of the target, this point will usually be the first place where the bird may be shot *comfortably*, i.e., the first place it may be shot without rushing.

**2:** With this vital index established we may now set up our feet. The shooter will place his left foot at approximately one o'clock to the intended killing-point and the right foot at three o'clock to it. The weight comes on to the ball of the leading left foot, the right heel is just coming off the ground.

**3:** The heel of the butt is positioned just below the armpit and the tip of the muzzles just below the line of sight to the target.

**4:** The shooter rotates the upper body and gun towards the trap, coming to rest at the point where the target first becomes clearly visible.

**5:** The bird is called for and as soon as it is in sight the upper body and gun start moving. The left hand brings the muzzles on to the bird. Smoothly, the gun comes up to the face and into the face and shoulder (the shoulder moving slightly forward to meet the gun) – the muzzles are now accelerating in front of the bird. The trigger is pulled as the gun comes into the face and shoulder and the right lead picture is seen.

**6:** The swing is then continued for a moment after the trigger is pulled to prevent the swing being checked. Throughout the shooting process the weight has remained on the left foot and focus has been on the bird with the muzzles being kept in peripheral vision.

As far as game shooting is concerned one does not have the luxury of being able to prepare oneself quite so methodically, one must anticipate a killing point and step into the bird's line, or, if one cannot move the feet, rely on good visual contact and an exaggerated rotation of the torso to get one in front of the target.

### The Churchill Method
Apart from being a famous gunmaker who popularised short barrelled shot-guns, Robert Churchill was famous in his day as an expert witness for Scotland Yard. There are two essential features to his shooting technique. The first is that the shooter should not consciously look for a lead picture, the second, the footwork.

The essential difference footwork-wise between Stanbury and Churchill is that with Churchill's style the feet are closer together, and the weight transfers on to a different foot depending on the shot. For a shot to the right the weight goes on to the right foot, for a shot to the left on to the left. In all cases the heel of the other foot rises as the shot is taken.

With Stanbury the weight always stays on the leading/left foot throughout the shooting process and whatever the shot. Moreover, with the Stanbury technique the body takes up a much more oblique stance. Churchill advocated standing almost square to the target. This of course has consequences on gun fit, as already noted, the Churchill shooter requiring a shorter gun with more cast, shorter because his shoulder starts further forward, more cast because his shoulder pocket is further out in relation to his eye and the rib.

Finally, a feature of the Churchill method which I often use for teaching beginners and which can be useful for gunfitting purposes, is the placement of the gun butt under the armpit as the shooter awaits the bird – the butt is gently squeezed between ribs and biceps. I have found this a very useful aid in good mounting technique and adopt it myself in modified form when shooting under FITASC 'gun down' rules. It forces the shooter to push the gun out, rather than drag it upwards. I find most beginners, and many experienced shots, mount more consistently with this technique, even though it does not look or feel particularly elegant.

## Fault Diagnosis

As well as the ability to understand and demonstrate various shooting methods, the aspiring shooting instructor or gunfitter must become expert in diagnosing flaws in a shooter's style. There is absolutely no point in adjusting a gun to shoot lower when the reason for the client's misses over the top are that his or her weight has come rearwards and that the head is therefore being lifted off the stock. It is beyond the scope of this book to consider fault diagnosis fully as it relates to style. It is enough to say that *where* someone is shooting is less important than *why* they are shooting there.

## Seeing the Shot

The ability to see shot in the air is a skill that gunfitters must acquire. It is much misunderstood. No-one sees the shot in the air for every shot, I would say most instructor gunfitters of the top flight see it 80 percent of the time, but are aware of the muzzle target relationship for every shot. Learning to see shot is a knack. One is not looking for individual pellets but a swarm, a dark mass, against the sky. To see it one should direct one's eye focus a few yards beyond the muzzles, and one must not be too close to the shooter, otherwise the view of the shot will be obscured by muzzle blast. The more you make an effort to see the shot the more often you will see it. You will find some brands of cartridges much easier to see than others.

## Equipment

Serious gunfitting calls both for specialised equipment and facilities, if the job is to be carried through successfully. The first requirement is a **safely positioned range** with a pattern plate, improvised or otherwise. If a pair of 6 ft square steel plates – the ideal – is not available, one may construct a temporary or permanent frame of wood or steel to which large sheets of paper or card may be pinned or clipped; however, an arrangement which offers a good frontal area and a solid backstop or adequate safety area to the rear is essential. If there is no backstop there must be a safety zone of 300 yards behind the plates or frame.

One does not fit on the patterning range alone, one will need to be able to present clay targets which will match the needs of the client. Game shooters being fitted for guns will require, as well as the usual crossers, quartering birds, rabbits and driven birds, some sort of 'walk-up', and a high tower – facilities which are not always available on the average sporting layout.

Game shooters may also require some sort of simulated grouse butt. Serious sporting shots will need to be presented with truly testing targets at the later stages in the fitting process. The needs of Skeet and Trap shots are more definable. If someone wants a gun fitted for English Skeet you will need an English Skeet range, if the interest is in Down the Line shooting, a DTL layout. Sometimes when the client is interested in the international disciplines, and the fitter's home range is unsuitable, fitter and client may need to travel to another range. One cannot properly fit a gun for Olympic Skeet shooting on an English Skeet range, nor is it any good fine tuning a gun destined for Olympic Trench competition on a Down the Line layout. The truly committed gunfitter will recognise these things and offer to travel when necessary, subject to expenses being re-imbursed.

I do not believe a *try gun* is essential equipment for a modern gunfitter involved mainly with the fitting of over-and-unders. If you do decide to buy a try gun be extremely careful. The few try guns which reach the open market tend to be poor buys: they are often over valued because of their rarity, and for obvious reasons, tend to be well used. One must, of course, check the condition of the bores and action as one would with any second-hand gun. Is there significant pitting? Have the bores been enlarged? Are they dented? Is the action tight on the face? What cartridges is the gun chambered for? There are some other special considerations concerning try gun purchase. What range of movements does the gun have? Are the mechanical elements of the stock mechanism prone to moving once they have been set? To test the latter point will require an extended live firing trial.

You may be saying 'what I need is a new try gun'. Be warned, however, that I have not yet seen a recently manufactured try gun of side-by-side or over-and-under pattern which was entirely satisfactory. There are some modern try guns of continental manufacture around, but all those that I have used have been both ungainly and prone to movement in the stock mechanism.

I am not saying that fitters should stay away from adjustable guns completely. An inexpensive and very practical alternative to the traditional try gun is to have a gun (I would suggest a Beretta 686 or a Browning 325) made up with one of Alan Rhone's adjustable combs and then fitted with one of the latest detachable recoil pads that allow one to interchange pads of different length. Such a set-up may not offer a full range of movements, but it is nevertheless most useful, especially as extremes of cast in over-and-unders are not advised. The particular advantage of Alan Rhone's comb conversion is that it allows for different adjustments of the comb at its front and rear, and it also allows for lateral movement. If one added a set of longer or shorter barrels (to achieve a set including both 28 and 30 in.) and some means of adjusting balance, such a gun would be superior to the traditional try gun. I am making up such a gun as this book goes to press. Similar conversions are available in the United States, where, in addition, at least one company, Reinhart Fajen of Warsaw, Missouri, offer complete try gun stocks for guns like the Remington 11–87.

Becoming expert in the *measuring of gun stocks* is a key skill for the gunfitter (and one which takes longer to master than might be imagined). To undertake the task the fitter will require a variety of measuring instruments. Some shooting schools have special stands for measuring guns. These fall into at least two types: very bulky Victorian and Edwardian measuring horses designed for use with side-by-sides, and moderately less bulky Italian machines designed for use with over-and-unders. In both the gun is firmly located by clamps; apart from giving confidence to clients, they greatly facilitate the process of accurate measurement – particularly of cast. They are not essential however, nor are specially constructed stock-length gauges, though such luxuries help to eliminate error and are time saving.

At the very least, a three foot or metre straight edge, a 6 and 12 in. steel rule and a retractable steel tape measure will be needed for measuring purposes. (Carpenter's callipers are also useful for measuring grip width and depth and stock and forend width.) The gunfitter will require a notebook, a supply of rubber butt extensions, comb raisers and the like. 'Blu-tack' or some other similar substance will also be useful for building up combs, as will 'moleskin' (otherwise intended for foot problems). Plastic electrician's tape and the wide, brown variety of adhesive packing tape should also form part of the gunfitter's standards kit as should a good pen or razor knife, a set of small turnscrews, snapcaps and all the safety equipment, clothing and other paraphernalia normally associated with shotgun shooting and instruction.

### Safety equipment
Be particularly attentive to the need for ear and eye protection for clients and yourself. The noise of the gun blast is greater for the instructor/fitter standing to one side of the client than it is for the client. Those who work with guns are also well advised to wear safety spectacles as a matter of routine; I know of several cases where eye injuries would have been avoided if they were worn. Steel shot is more dangerous than lead shot when being shot at plates because it is more prone to ricochet. Carrying on with the safety theme, many instructors and gunfitters opt for electronic muffs: they offer excellent hearing protection and do not impede communication. All shooting instructors and gunfitters should have some knowledge of first aid, and carry with them a first aid kit (which if nothing else will come in useful when people close their fingers in guns or mangle them on top-levers). Every gunfitter should also be insured.

### Getting on with the Job
Assuming we have the right facilities and equipment, and a reasonable grasp of the theory behind gunfit, how do we actually set about gun-fitting?

Ideally we will first apprentice ourselves to someone who has the benefit of years of experience. Such opportunities are not always available, however, so I will lay out here the sort of procedure which I would regard as ideal. However, this no more than a rough guide.

First we must introduce ourselves to the client. It is crucial that a good relationship be established from the start. However, do not be too laid back in your approach (even if you are gunfitting as an amateur). A little formality is usually appropriate, not least because one of the first things we should discuss with any client we do not know is safety (I would suggest something along the lines of 'Hello . . . . . . I'm [your name], your instructor/gunfitter. We'll be working together this morning/afternoon. Before we consider any-thing else just a word on safety . . . '). It has to be said that as far as gunfitters and safety are concerned familiarity can breed contempt. As someone who has *very* nearly been shot twice (not whilst fitting or instructing), I never skimp on safety. I pass this on to readers of this book: overcome your embarrassment, be kind, be polite, but be a stickler for safety. What you teach to your clients will be passed on by them to other shooters, a positive chain is created. Conversely if you let a point of safety slip by, you are abandoning your duty and may responsible for an accident in the future, you might even be the victim of it.

After explaining in a firm and friendly way the potential hazards of shoot-ing, one should go on to discuss with the client the sort of shooting he or she is planning to do. As we do this, we shall begin to form an impression of the person and their experience. Always keep in mind that unlimited patience and a sense of humour are essential attributes for any instructor or gunfitter (not to mention enthusiasm, knowledge and authority). When one has to deal with a really difficult client – as one sometimes inevitably will – one must bite one's tongue and, hopefully, win them over by a clearly superior understanding of the subject. Sometimes it does not work and one must live with it and just maintain a professional approach.

Our next task is to ask the client whether they suffer from any eyesight problems. Look and see if the client is wearing contact lenses. You may find it useful to have some sort of basic eye test chart on a wall. One cannot over emphasise the importance of eyes in shooting, a new pair of glasses or contact lens prescribed by a practically-minded optometrist (every gunfitter should strike up a relationship with one) can transform shooting perfor-mance.

Once we are satisfied that the client has no hidden deficiencies of sight, we may progress to asking if they are right- or left-handed, and from there to a test for eye dominance. The identification of a shooter's master eye is a critical consideration in shotgun marksmanship and gunfitting and worthy of the extended comment it is about to get – I know of many cases of eyesight anomalies being incorrectly diagnosed by instructors and fitters who should have been more careful.

There are a variety of ways of testing for eye dominance; I believe the best test is with a gun, because it tells the fitter most about the client's vision. However, I note that recently there has been some ill-informed criticism of this method on safety grounds. Carried out by someone who is aware of, and respects, the lethal potential of firearms, it is safe.

## Methods of Testing for Eye Dominance

*Method 1: with a gun*
Get the client to mount the gun and aim at the instructor/fitter's master eye (which the latter should indicate with the tip of his index finger). It goes without saying that both fitter and client will have first *checked that the gun is unloaded* (moreover, explain to the client that this is a special circumstance – the only time it is permissible to break the first rule of gun safety).

If the client has a master eye which corresponds to his hand dominance, it will be immediately clear to the fitter because his eye will be looking along the rib; if, on the other hand, his eye and hand dominance are opposite, this will also be immediately clear. Although the gun is mounted on one shoulder, it will be evident that the 'wrong' eye is being used for sighting, pulling the muzzles out of line. If the client has central vision, where neither eye is fully dominant, it will appear that the muzzles are in line with the bridge of the nose. Other variations of eye dominance are possible which are considered later in more detail.

*Method 2: by making a circle with the thumb and forefinger.*
(a) As with 1, indicate to the client your master eye with the tip of your index finger. Ask them to make a circle by touching the tips of their thumb and index finger together. Then ask them to focus on your fingertip and bring the circle they have created up into their line of vision. You will see if either eye is dominant and you will also be able to detect anomalies falling between total right or total left dominant vision most easily with this technique.
(b) For self-testing, use procedure as at 4 below.

*Method 3: with a piece of card with a hole in it*
Take a piece of card about six inches square with a 1 in. circular hole in the middle. Ask the client to look at your master eye (indicated as above). Now ask the client to look at it through the hole in the card, holding the card at arm's length. The eye chosen for this task will, almost invariably, be the master eye. The diagnosis is confirmed by asking the client to 'keep looking at my fingertip but bring the card up to your face'. They will usually bring the card back to their master eye, a few will hesitate, trying to look through the hole with both eyes. Hesitation or the attempt to look through the hole with both eyes may be an indication of central vision or other anomaly.

*Method 4: with a cardboard tube such as found in the centre of a roll of kitchen paper*
A simple method useful for self-testing. Identify an object on the horizon and, holding the tube in the preferred hand, bring it up into the line of sight, centring the object in it. Close the eye on the same side as the preferred hand. Is the object still centred? If not, your hand and eye dominance are probably the same.

*Method 5: with a large piece of thick paper rolled into a cone*
As suggested by John Brindle.

Give the client a cone like a dunce's cap which you have formed from a large sheet of paper (Brindle recommends 3 by 4 ft). A hole about 1 in. wide is required in the 'pointed end', the opposite end should be about 15 in. in diameter. The client is asked to hold the cone with both hands immediately to their front so that they are looking into the large end. With the fitter standing about 9 or 10 ft away, they are then asked to look through the hole at the fitter's master eye, which is indicated with a finger tip. Most people will be seen to centre one eye – their master eye – perfectly in the centre of the cone. However some will locate the eye to one side as they look and some will use one eye and then the other. To quote John Brindle, 'The latter, when the observer comes closer, so arrange the cone that from the observer's point of view it is the bridge of their nose which occupies the centre of the circle.' These individuals may well have central vision.

*Method 6: with a plastic or wooden pistol with a 1 in. ring as a foresight and no backsight*
The mock pistol; with its ring sight is used as are the fingers in Method 2. This method was invented by Chris Cradock. It is entertaining and informative, showing clearly conditions not simply categorised as full dominance. Chris likes the client to use their weak hand to hold the pistol and he also likes them to stand as they would when they shoot.

*Method 7: with no props*
Ask the client to point at an object with his or her index finger, keeping both eyes open and, once the client is pointing at it, ask them to shut or cover their left eye (right eye for left-handers). Now ask, 'Has your finger moved?'. If the answer is 'no', nine times out of ten all is well: hand and eye dominance are the same. But if the answer is 'yes', the client probably has opposite hand and eye dominance. Confirm the diagnosis by getting the client to point a finger at your master eye – if he or she is 'wrong' eye dominant, or if neither eye is dominant, it will (usually) be apparent to you.

*Method 8: with the fitter/instructor standing behind the client*
The client is positioned to face several evenly spaced numbers on the horizon such as those found above the targets on some rifle ranges.

The client is asked to point at a number with his or her gun normally mounted. Looking over the shoulder of the client, the fitter is immediately aware of gross master eye problems.

PLATE 11     Right and left eye dominance and central vision.

Making an alteration to a Boss try gun. Note the single trigger for which Boss is famous.

Paul Roberts, Chairman of John Rigby & Co, measuring drop at comb and heel.

*(below, left)* An Italian jig used by Gunmark, the Beretta importers in the United Kingdom, for measuring over-and-unders. This modern device is one of the most accurate yet devised for measuring gun stocks. *(below, right)* Another measuring device, this one used at the shooting grounds of the London gunmakers Boss.

A precise diagnosis of eye dominance is crucial. I include these various methods so that you may experiment in this area and find out what works best for you and your clients. My own favourites are 1 and 2.

We have tested for eye dominance, what next? We use the information gained. A right-hander with a left master eye (or a left-hander with a right master eye) has a number of options. The best is to learn to shoot from the opposite shoulder. I teach hundreds of people to shoot each year, and have found this to be by far the most effective course for most of those who have eyesight anomalies. It allows full use of one's binocular vision. However, not everyone will want to change shoulders, and for those with central vision it will be no solution anyway. The remaining courses of action are to block the vision to one eye by some means, to use a gun with a cross-over (sometimes called cross-eye) stock or, occasionally it may be possible to retrain shooter's eyes. (There needs to be more experiment in this area; one technique which seems to work with those who wear glasses is to have a prescription lens on only the side which one wants to be dominant.)

## Blocks to vision
Perhaps the simplest remedy for any eyesight anomaly relating to dominance is to get in the habit of closing or dimming the eye on the shoulder opposite the gun stock. It should be noted however that one need only close or dim the eye a moment before the trigger is pulled, this allows one to get the benefits of binocular vision as one locks onto the target visually, but ensures (if one remembers to do it) that there is no confusing image when the trigger is pulled.

Another way to get around eyesight problems is to shoot wearing an eye-patch, or, if one wears spectacles, with a translucent barrier over the appropriate lens. A variation on this theme is for the fitter to carefully place a dot on the client's spectacles precisely in line with the line of vision of the offending eye. This will have a similar effect to winking just before the trigger is pulled. The dot, which should be no more than ½ in. in diameter, will not significantly impede normal vision but it will block the image of the offending eye at the critical moment. The dot may be made using something like typing correction fluid (which is easily scraped off when dry with a finger nail) or sticky tape. Once correctly position it may be made permanent by sandblasting or otherwise frosting the area marked out. Beware that if the small dot system is to work, and it is *very* effective, the glasses being used must locate positively on the shooters head. The 'aviation' frames with curled wire side pieces are ideal for the purpose.

There are other more curious options for sorting out master eye problems: side-by-side users may equip their barrels with a small barrier to vision, a so called 'obdurator' on a specially adapted handguard. A similar system may be applied to over-and-unders (a device called a 'blocker' which attaches to the rib near the muzzles is available in the States for over-and-unders and repeaters). Another strange device is the Monopeian sight once sold by W.W. Greener[2]. Those who have no special fondness for Heath Robinson impedimenta, might consider the Robert Churchill method, raising the thumb of the hand supporting the forend hand in the manner of an obdurator or blocker attached to the gun.[3]

Which one of all these systems is best? I have already stated my preference for teaching people to shoot off the opposite shoulder whenever possible. Closing or dimming one eye is also simple and effective, but my normal second course of action for those with eye problems is the use of spectacles with the small dot placed as described earlier. Some people find it hard to close one eye, even those who are comfortable with the procedure may sometimes forget to close the appropriate eye.

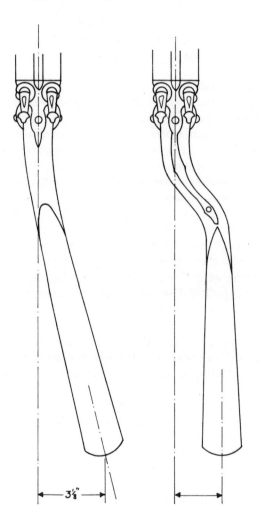

Crossover stocks, one with extreme cast, one with dog leg. I am not fond of these stocks, and believe most shooters afflicted with master eye problems are better advised to learn to shoot off the opposite shoulder, to equip themselves with a barrier to vision in the offending eye or to squint or close one eye, after making initial visual contact with the target.

3⅛"

**Crossover stocks**

The expensive option for dealing with cross dominance is to acquire a gun with a crossover stock – a gun which has extreme cast usually achieved by bending the action and blending it into a stock with a very obvious S bend in it (these guns allow the shooter to mount the gun on one shoulder whilst using the eye of the opposite side)[4]. I am no great fan of such guns, especially if the principle is applied to the over-and-unders, but some instructors still believe in them, and without doubt measuring up for one is a real test of a fitter's skill.

J.H. Walsh explained the thinking behind crossover guns more than a hundred years ago: 'The usual practice is to cast off the stock . . . a little more than the space between the centres of the two eyes . . . [thus enabling] the left eye to take aim along the barrel. On measuring the space between the eyes, it will be found to average 2½ in., but by adjusting the head to the line of sight, less than this may in some cases suffice, and in some cases fairly good shooting has been obtained with a cast-off of less than half that amount. But, it will be found that the gun stocked in this way shoots considerably to the left of aim, owing to the left hand giving way, and in so doing the stock bruises the cheek. Hence I have almost always heard from left-eyed men that they could do best with a full 3 in. deviation of the stock to the left [which remains a typical cast at heel measurement for a cross over gun].' Gough Thomas has noted that any tendency of a crossover gun to shoot in the direction opposite to the cast because of the unusual line of recoil force may be counteracted by flex in the grip. Practically, I find crossover guns are awkward to use and tend to recoil excessively.

**Eyesight – Conclusions**

There is more to the question of eye dominance than the simple discovery that someone is right or left eye dominant or indeed that they have 'central vision'. Some will have one eye only slightly more dominant than the other, others will have one eye much more dominant but still not absolutely. Anything other than full eye dominance corresponding to the individual's handedness will have the effect of pulling the muzzles to one side of the target if the shooter habitually keeps both eyes open. The subtle variations of eye dominance require experience to spot. You may see, for example, when applying the methods mentioned earlier that the shooter has a tendency to raise their gun/finger slightly off line momentarily before coming into line as if they were being distracted by the other eye. Beware of these shooters. What seems a very slight tendency when testing can translate to a very significant error at targets. If someone seems to repeatedly shoot up the side of some targets consider testing their eye dominance again, even if you had them down as simply right or left dominant.

In the old days some gunmakers used to adjust cast rather liberally to accommodate eye dominance problems such as central vision. I believe that guns should, usually, only be altered for such conditions after very careful consideration. Eye dominance can change: most instructors know of cases where middle-aged men have had dramatic changes in eye dominance. Moreover long distance driving, habitual staring at a computer screen, and simple fatigue can all effect eye dominance. Some people's eye dominance is also affected by the high 'stacked-barrel' profile of the over-and-unders, which can distract the weak eye on some shots. The only really reliable test of shooting eyesight is to observe a person shooting on several different occasions with these things in mind. No-one can write down rules which will work in every case. Some might disagree, but I also feel that short barrelled guns are less forgiving of minor eye dominance anomalies than long barrelled guns. Finally, on the subject of female shooters, be aware that the majority have some degree of cross dominance.

## NOTES

1   With the experienced shooter, who has learnt how to mount the gun, this order might be reversed, drop is the critical measurement. Length, whilst still important, is less important to someone who does not find the act of mounting awkward.

2   The Monopeian sight involved the attachment of two protrusions from the barrels each with a sighting triangle. I have also heard of a similar system involving two clips to the barrels, one at the muzzles, one at the forend, each with a rod projecting out about 3 in. tipped by a small globe sight.

3   The thumbstall system is also mentioned by Teasedale-Buckell in his *Experts on Guns and Shooting*.

4   The principle may also be used in less extreme form to create a semi-crossover stock for those with central vision. In the United States a different style of 'cross-over' stock is very occasionally seen, where, instead of having a stock with a dog leg, the stock is massively scooped and twisted so that the head may be laid almost flat. I have not had the chance to shoot such a gun, but it certainly looks ungainly and I would suspect it is awkward to use as well.

# 6

# USING THE TRY GUN

So, we have briefed the client on safety (if we think it is necessary), we have formed some sort of preliminary opinion on their level of competence, having talked to them and watch them mount a gun, and we have ascertained their dominant eye. What next? That will depend on whether we want to use a try gun or not. If we do, which means we will have a try gun in our possession which corresponds to type of gun that client is intending to use (I think it bad practice to fit someone who is about to buy an over-and-under with a side-by-side try gun), we may set up the try gun's stock to what we think are the approximate dimensions required. These will initially be based on observation of the shooter's physique and any peculiarities of style we may have already noted.

Having set the gun up roughly, the fitter will then hand it to the client – *having demonstrated to his own and the client's satisfaction that the weapon is unloaded* – and ask the client to mount the gun. Necessary adjustments will be made, in the order length, cast and drop at heel, pitch, and cast and drop at face, with the client mounting the gun several times and the fitter observing and modifying fit thereafter.

The fitter will need to walk a pace or two ahead of the client, and, having already explained to the client the very special circumstance, ask them to point the (*proven empty*) gun at his (the fitter's) eye. To avoid confusion the fitter will indicate which eye (his master) by placing the tip of his index finger beneath it. This process will almost certainly be repeated a couple of times with small adjustments being made after each before moving on to a live firing trial at the pattern plates. (However, do not spend too much time on dry fitting or you may lose the client's interest). At the plates further adjustments will be made to the gun dependent upon the results of actual shooting.

Some points worth bearing in mind are:

**1:** The fitter, who is responsible for safety, should load for the client (indeed I always prefer to keep all cartridges in my possession during any instructional or fitting session).

**2:** Each time the client fires, the fitter should physically take charge of the gun, unless the intention is immediately to fire again.

**3:** Because some try guns are a bit long in the tooth, and because it is possible for their mechanism to be affected by recoil, some shooting grounds use only lightly loaded 'training' cartridges in them.

**4:** There must be a clear aiming mark on the plates or pattern sheet.

**5:** For the first shot or two at the plates or sheet, the gun should be premounted as in trap shooting (you should ask the client to mount the gun at about 45 degrees into the sky and bring the mounted gun down to the horizontal); later, the client should be encouraged to shoot at the mark less deliberately (some experienced shooters, when shooting from a pre-mounted position, naturally adjust their eye to be in line with the rib whatever the stock; this can of course mask problems of gunfit).

**6:** The range for conducting these trials at plates should be between 16 and 40 yards. My own preference is to start close – 16 yards – it makes it easier to immediately determine the centre of the pattern and saves walking backwards and forwards with the client, but I also like to have a final check, when gun and client as a unit seem 'on the money', at 40 yards.

**7:** At 16 yards, an adjustment of ⅛ in. is going to cause a shift in impact of about two inches – such is the theory at least, but wait and see just how great the effect of small changes can be in practice.

**8:** Unless the problem is a gross one (which it should not be if you have taken time to fit the client 'dry'), never adjust the gun on the result of just one or two shots; rather wait for the client to shoot at least three or four shells.

**9:** Be attentive to faults in the client's style which may be causing a shift in impact – we have already noted that one should always be extremely reluctant to alter a gun to compensate for bad technique.

Once everything seems about right on the plates, with the gun printing its pattern one-third below and two-thirds above the point of aim (or as required)[1], it is time to move on to shoot some clays for confirmation and fine tuning according to individual style. The first bird should be a simple, slow, approaching target at moderate height, since this is one of the easiest shots for most people. If the client seems to have no obvious problems here move on to a going away shot. This is a most useful target for gunfitting purposes and may be used both to check drop and cast. With this target my procedure is normally to start fairly close to the trap and, once the target is being broken consistently, to move gradually backwards to make the bird harder.

There are other targets which are especially useful in a gunfitting session. The fast bird driven immediately overhead and fast but close crossers are useful for checking the length of the stock (too long a stock will, very obviously, impede both shots). High driven birds are useful for checking cast because lateral aiming errors are easily picked up. High crossing and quartering targets are very useful for checking pitch. Too little pitch will make it harder to keep up on the line of the bird. Once one has gone through the basics, it is all up to the experience of the fitter and the wishes of the client. It goes without saying that targets in any fitting session should be varied, corresponding to the type of target that the shooter is most likely to engage with the gun: one can not fit someone for a trap gun properly on a skeet range.

Do not assume that your diagnosis of the client's master eye was correct. Some people will seem to change eye dominance on certain targets. I am afflicted with this problem. As a right-handed, normally right-master-eyed shot, I sometimes have difficulty on high quartering targets from the left. It took me a long time to discover it was because my eye dominance sometimes changed on this shot, the left eye taking over because it was seeing the target first. Ken Davies has noted the same problem and suggests that it is aggravated by wide-set eyes, and or a style in which the arms are used to move the gun rather than rotation of the upper torso. Ken also notes that canting of the head and the relative raising of one eye it causes may be a factor. One thing which can certainly aggravate the problem is gun which is set too low, so that the right eye is effectively blocked by the view of the breech thus forcing the left eye to take over. The simple remedy for those who would *otherwise* shoot well is to blink the left eye on this target.

When fitter and client are satisfied one should make a final record of the dimensions of the try gun on a standardised form.

## Gunfitting without a Try Gun
There is much to be said for and much to be learnt from gunfitting without a try gun. As already noted, nearly all try guns suffer from a rather awkward balance and a rather strange feel in the grip. Moreover, guns are such singular objects that what applies to one is unlikely to apply precisely to another. These things, together with the fact that the shooter wants to be fitted to the gun he or she is actually going to use and the scarcity of good over-and-under try guns lead me to do most of my own gunfitting without a try gun.

If you choose not to use a try gun, whether by choice or necessity, you must make sure that the client begins a fitting session with a gun which is, or can easily be adapted to, a tolerable fit. Just what is tolerable? It would make little sense to start off with a 14 in. stock for someone of 6 ft 4 in., or ½ in. of cast for someone with narrow shoulders and a thin face. Nevertheless, it is all too common to come across shooters struggling with grossly ill-fitting guns. The fitter's problems really mount up when someone has adapted to an ill-fitting gun. The problem is that a better fitting gun will, initially, feel wrong to these clients. You must use all your powers of persuasion to convince the client that a significant change will help in the long run. Sometimes you will just have to accept that you are fitting a gun to someone who will always have a less than perfect style.

If you are using the client's own gun in a fitting session, you should start proceedings – after the normal safety lecturette and eyesight checks – by measuring it up and recording the results in your fitting notebook or diary. This gets one thinking about the gun, and creates a record of measurements which can be referred to in the future: especially useful when a gun goes away to a stocker and comes back wrongly altered (which happens more often than you might think).

From here on, the procedure is very similar to that with a try gun, except that one must use a little extra ingenuity. If the gun is a multi-choke type, use the tightest chokes available in order to make shifts in point of impact more obvious. If the client has their own gun watch them shooting it before making any adjustments; if you are providing the gun, get the drop right by sight as described in Chapter 4 and adjust the length for a two finger nose to base of thumb gap before going to the plates. You can lengthen the stock with a pad, or build up the comb with a rubber comb raiser (available in at least three sizes from better gun shops) or strips of card or putty under electrical or packing tape. One cannot do much about cast, but it is the least important of the main variables anyway. 'Ah,' I can hear you saying, 'but what happens if you need to get rid of wood?' The answer, I am afraid, is that you cannot (although you may be able to remove a butt plate or recoil pad to reduce length, which may have a marginal effect on cast as well). Most gunfitters seem to manage! Ideally, the modern gunfitter would include in his kit several different stocks for each of the more common over-and-unders; these might be equipped with adjustable combs and recoil pad.

The secret of making temporary adjustments on a gun is to take a little extra care over them. Do not leave a surface which is going to drag on skin or clothing, or a temporary addition which is going to drop off at the least convenient moment. Slip-on rubber recoil pads and rubber comb raisers can be a dreadful nuisance unless they are properly taped up (I like to use black or brown plastic electrician's tape: it does not distract the eye, and it is fairly kind to most stock finishes – however, care should still be exercised when removing it).

Finally, a reminder on the instructor/fitter's manner, which applies to gunfitting in all circumstances. The tone of voice should be friendly but, when required, firm. You must be in control, and you must inspire confidence in a quiet authoritative way. An instructor/fitter who gives the impression either of indecision or arrogance is not going to succeed. If a client is not confident in the fitter, he will not be confident of the fit, and that can have disastrous consequences on shooting performance. Of rather more importance is the fact that if you lose or fail to gain control of the gunfitting situation, someone may get killed, quite possibly you.

## NOTES

1  Always remember, patterning figures like one-third or two-thirds are no more than a starting point. I noted earlier that for sporting and skeet use I prefer a gun – if it is an over-and-under – which shoots very nearly, but not quite, flat. Other people have different preferences: some skeet shooters like a high shooting gun, especially those who are practitioners of Olympic skeet where there can be a tendency to chop

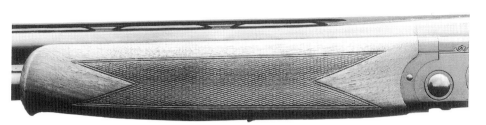

A schnabel forend on a Beretta 682 Supersports.

A plain but elegant and practical forend on a Beretta 686.

A forend with finger grooves on a Miroku shotgun.

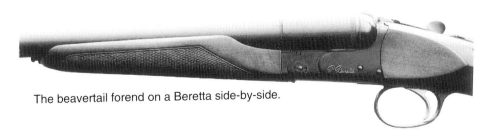

The beavertail forend on a Beretta side-by-side.

PLATE 13

The gunfitter strives to create a gun which is a natural extension of arms and eyes.

PLATE 16

through the line of the bird because of the speed of gun mounting; a gun which shoots slightly high can compensate for this. Many trap shooters like a fairly high shooting gun (their starting position over the trap house will affect their drop requirement, as will the speed with which they take their first shot). The advantage of high shooting guns, as we have discussed, is that it gives a bit of a built-in lead on rising birds; it also allows the target to be kept in sight more easily throughout the process of shooting. Some shooters will not want this. It does not, for example, suit my own style of shooting Down the Line. I like a fairly flat shooting gun for sporting and, unusually, for DTL. I take the first shot at trap very quickly, almost blotting out the target, and, if I need a second shot, I also prefer a flat shooting gun because the target is likely to be dropping. As far as game shooting is concerned, I enjoy shooting a side-by-side, but when I shoot a side-by-side I adopt a less deliberate and more instinctive style than with my clay shooting, and find that a traditional one-third: two-thirds pattern placement is just right. Experiment and experience leads me to believe that a technique of aiming which tends towards the deliberate, in which there may be some conscious awareness of the foresight, may cause the muzzles to raise slightly in relation to the target compared to an instinctive forget-about-lead-keep-your-eyes-glued-on-the-target-approach. In other words I think that a maintained lead shot may well shoot with less of a gap between bird and bead than a practitioner of the Churchill method, and therefore require a slightly different gunfit for drop. We have already noted that side-by-sides may require less drop because of their down flip in the first phase of recoil.

# 7

# OBSERVATIONS

This is the section of the book in which I include the information that did not easily fit elsewhere. It is a collection of observations, some of them reinforcing points made earlier.

**Preconceptions**
Start with no ideal measurements in mind, the right measurements are those which suit the individual's physique and style.

**Length: Trap Guns**
Trap shooters are often given a slightly longer (¼ to ½ in.) gun than game, sporting or skeet shooters. The rationale for this is that their gun is premounted and therefore a longer gun, which has certain sighting advantages, can be advocated without any negative side-effects. In the United States however there is a school of thought championed by phenomenal trap shot Kay Ohye which favours short stocks for trap.

**The Weight of Guns and Length** – traditional lore
Very heavy guns, for example big bore wildfowling pieces, are usually made short in the stock and thick in the grip (when one handles the old monsters, they do not feel short – which I suppose only proves the point). Conversely, very light small-bore guns should – according to traditional thought – be made slightly longer in the stock because they are easier to handle, a little extra length makes them steadier.

**How Length affects Drop**
Adding length to a stock which has a normal inclined comb increases drop, because it brings the face back to a lower point on the comb. Shortening a stock tends to decrease drop, because it brings the face forward to a higher point on the comb.

**How Cast affects Drop**
It should be clear by now that all the variables we have discussed can effect each other. Just as length can affect drop so can cast. If one adds cast to a gun, it can cause the sighting eye to drop in relation to the rib, because the position of the cheek bone on the comb is altered.

In the same way that adding cast to a gun effectively decreases comb height, reducing cast effectively increases the comb height. The cheekbone is pushed up as the stock is pushed closer towards the axis of the rib.

### Barrel length and Drop

A long barrelled gun may need less drop than a short barrelled gun fitted for the same shooter. Long barrels, especially on a side-by-side, can make a gun shoot low (short barrels are stiffer and therefore less prone to down flip).

### Barrel Length and Physique

One might be tempted to say that common sense suggests that a short man will be better suited to short barrels and a tall man better suited to long ones. It might even appear that it would be sensible to suggest that barrel length should always be in proportion to the user's physique. It would be dangerous to make such a statement, however! Although someone of 6 ft 4 in. looks distinctly odd with a Churchill XXV (25 in.) gun, many sporting clay shooters, even those of modest stature, find there is a distinct advantage in using 32 in. barrelled guns and do not look notably overgunned when handling them. The longer guns point well, and the extra mass in the barrels helps the shooter to follow through consistently. However, I must also add that I think those who shoot infrequently are better off with the shorter barrelled gun. They are a more instinctive tool.

### Women

There are a number of special gunfit considerations with regard to women. I might start by repeating the fact most right-handed women do not have full right eye dominance. Although I often succeed in getting a man with cross-dominance to shoot off the opposite shoulder, I have found this much more difficult with women. Many women also find it hard to close one eye, so a block to the vision of one eye may well be the only answer.

As far as guns are concerned, many will suggest that women should use lighter guns; it all depends on the women in question. Most women, like most men, are perfectly capable of using a normal twelve bore. All the smaller gauges and bores (with the possible exception of the magnum 20-bores) have a built-in disadvantage: they throw a smaller charge, and therefore require more accurate shot placement. Moreover, the lack of weight is itself a disadvantage in clay shooting where a reasonably heavy gun is required to promote steadiness of swing and reduce recoil.

However, any gun, and particularly the 12-bore, will generally need to be adapted for female use. Most guns manufactured today have butt plates designed for men with relatively flat chests. Women, especially those with large breasts, will need a gun with a well rounded toe (see below). I might also note here that breast-feeding mothers, who may have a temporarily enlarged bosom, should not attempt to adjust their gun for their condition, but should temporarily refrain from shooting.

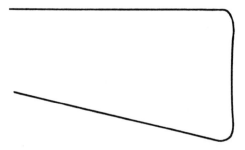

A lady's butt.

## Children

Young shots, and anyone else of really small stature will not only require shorter gun stocks, but a stock in proportion to their general physique. For example, it is no good merely sawing a couple of inches off a butt to fit a boy or girl if the grip is proportioned for an adult hand. When cutting down stocks it is always a good idea to keep the off-cut so that in future years a stock may be lengthened easily. As we have noted, it is likely that young people will require a higher stock comb on average than adults because the distance between their eye socket and cheekbone is smaller.

## Disabled Shooters

The needs of disabled shooters vary a great deal; creating guns to suit their needs is a wonderful challenge to the professional fitter. The fitter is likely to come into contact with at least two groups of disabled shooters, those with missing arms, hands or fingers, and the wheelchair bound. The first category will require, above all else a gun which they can grip and open easily. Modifications to both grip and top lever may therefore be called for. If the gun is a side-by-side, easy opening may be a useful feature. Whatever the barrel configuration it may make sense to keep the stock a little heavier than normal so the gun is easier to swing. Right-handed shooters with an artificial left hand may require a modified forend. Single trigger guns will make sense for one armed game shooters (which is not to say that some have not made very effective use of double triggers). Wheelchair bound shooters present a different set of problems. Much will depend on whether or not they have full use of their upper body. Those restricted in this respect may prefer a faster handling gun. Because anyone in a sitting position is forced to shoot with more arm movement and less torso rotation, a shorter gun stock may also be useful. Guns which recoil less are also advisable, because the body does not operate as effectively as a shock absorber when seated.

## Ribs

Quite a lot has been written about ribs over the years, as far as their size and shape is concerned, but very little has been said about the much more

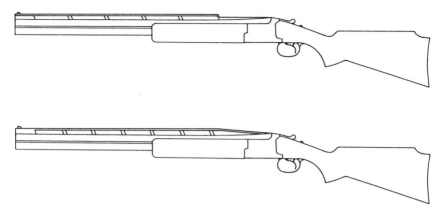

Two high-ribbed guns, one with a stepped rib, the other with an
exaggerated ramp sometimes seen on American trap guns.

important subject of their pitch relative to the bore axis. My own research
leads me to believe that in many mass-produced guns rib pitch is incorrect. Although it is not easily altered, it is an important variable in gunfit.
One may experiment to a degree with this variable by use of an add-on
rib. I have used an aluminium strip for this purpose, packed to varying
degrees at the muzzle. I bond it to the original rib with a contact adhesive
like 'Evostick', after experimenting one may easily remove both rib and
glue.[1]

*High ribs:* Although they are often fitted to trap guns, high or raised ribs
have a tendency to make a gun shoot low (if they are high at both muzzle and
breech). Generally, makers compensate for extra-high ribs – which some
shooters like, because the rib drops the barrels out of the field of vision – by
means of a raised comb. High ribs and high combs suit some shooters.
However, for others, high ribs, especially the ultra-high, stepped types, can
distract the eye and are less natural to point.

*Tapered ribs:* The style and width of the rib should be agreeable to the user.
On over-and-unders I think a plain flat 10 mm rib is perfectly adequate, but I
also like a slightly tapered rib with a narrow, shallow centre channel. Ribs
are very personal. It is sometimes suggested that the tapered rib draws the
eye to the target more effectively than other types (which of course is ideal;
what is wanted is a rib which remains in peripheral vision but which does
not distract the shooter from keeping his or her focus on the target). My
experience supports this point of view. Some tapered ribs also create a visual
illusion which can be useful for gunfitting purposes: they appear to make
barrels longer (which is why Robert Churchill used a narrow tapered rib on
his 25 in. barrelled guns).

### Vibration – a Hidden Variable

Both the density of the wood used in the stock of a gun, the steel used in its barrels and the thickness of barrels and action can effect the vibration characteristics of a gun, as can the design of the stock and barrels. Vibration can cause problems which are often very difficult to trace. I am reminded of one gun, a 32 in. trap gun converted into a sporter, which I could never get to feel quite right when shot. Eventually, I could only conclude that the lack of density of the stock wood, and the straight grain of the wood combined with the 'humming' of the long, hard steel, machine-made barrels, was causing the problem. The great shot of the Victorian and Edwardian era, Lord Walsingham apparently objected to steel barrels on the grounds of their 'ringing', and, remained loyal to his trusty Damascus tubes throughout his life. Vibration requires better study. My subjective impression is that well-figured, dense gun stocks, well-fitted at the head, reduce shock transmission to the face and shoulder.

### Barrel Regulation

Another factor which can lead to problems is barrel regulation. Most twelve bore guns are regulated to 40 yards: that is, the point of impact of the two barrels should coincide at that distance. But, in practice, some guns do not shoot as they should. For example, many over-and-unders have a tendency to throw their top barrel pattern high (a factor which is usually related to a different point of inertia at the shoulder for the top barrel rather than a simple geometrical error in barrel alignment or, as described above, because they are equipped with an improperly pitched rib). The moral is: *never assume that a gun is properly regulated*. As a matter of course, the regulation of a competition gun should, like its nominal chokings, always be checked (and never by a third party, but by the user if need be supervised by his or her fitter). If the regulation of a gun is faulty, and the point of impact of the two barrels significantly different, it can lead to no end of confusion. If the gun is fitted for one barrel only one is asking for problems. A good barrel maker may be able to adjust faulty regulation by choke or bore adjustment; re-regulation involving movement of the barrel tubes is a major and expensive operation. A final point: some trap guns are designed to shoot the second barrel low, because by the time the second shot is needed, it is assumed that the target will be dropping.

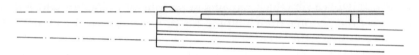

Barrel and rib regulation in the vertical plane. The angle of the rib is an important, but rarely considered variable.

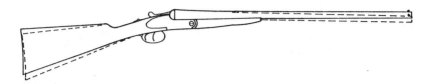

Barrel and stock flexure in the first phase of recoil in a side-by-side gun.

## Recoil

Recoil may be considered (simplifying somewhat) in two phases. During the first the gun comes back and may flex in both vertical and horizontal planes. In the second phase the gun, if it is traditionally stocked, will rotate at the shoulder (more drop at heel will cause more rotation) and the angle of the comb relative to the face will change.

## Excessive Recoil

I believe that in years to come, we will discover that recoil is far more dangerous than we realise at present. Reasons for excessive recoil may include: too short or long a gun; a comb which slopes up too much or excessive drop, excessive cast; a light-weight gun; an unsuitable cartridge/gun combination; a gun which is 'off the face' – i.e., in which the barrels and action are not properly jointed; a gun in which wood to metal fit between action and butt is poor; a gun which has excessive headspace in the chamber; a gun which has chambers which are too large; a gun which has been too tightly bored; a gun which has short forcing cones in front of its chambers; tight choking; a gun with a grip shape which is inappropriate and prevents the rear hand firmly holding the gun; and, not least, a gun which is being mounted incorrectly. In my experience, however, the two most common causes of excessive felt recoil in guns of average weight, using normal cartridges, are *comb angle* and *bore diameter*.

## Recoil Brakes, Reducers and Pads

Recoil brakes are not particularly common in the United Kingdom but are very popular in the United States. The old type of recoil brake was typified by the famous 'Cutt's Compensator'. More recently, many guns have been 'ported'. That is, they have had holes or slots cut into their muzzles to direct propellant gases in such a fashion that they counteract the upward flip of the gun in recoil. These devices can be effective, with the aid of slow motion photography one can see that upward movement of the muzzles may be reduced as much as fifty percent, causing a reduction in felt recoil because the gun does not rotate at the shoulder as much as it might, and hence, relatively, the comb stays flatter in recoil. However, they have the notable disadvantage of directing propellant gases and muzzle blast closer to the

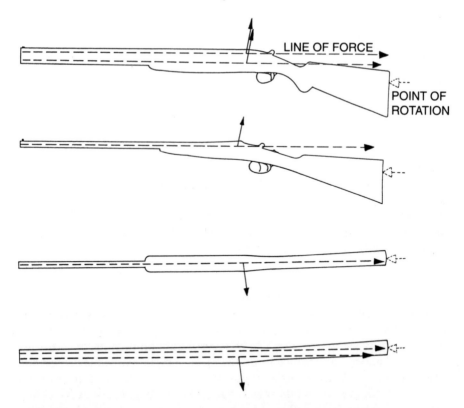

Although sufficient experiment is yet to be carried out, my observation is that over-and-unders tend to shoot higher than side-by-sides, especially as far the top barrel is concerned. The higher line of the top barrel is one obvious reason why the dip effect is increased, but reduced barrel flex in the vertical plane may also be a significant factor in their higher shooting. Over-and-unders and side-by-sides also seem to react differently to recoil in the horizontal plane. In an over-and-under with average cast the butt sole is out of line with the line of the barrels; this is not the case as far as the right barrel of a cast-off side-by-side is concerned. In this case the right-hand edge of the comb is more or less in line with the right barrel. Over-and-unders do not seem to react well to extremes of cast. The stiffness of their thicker grips may be another factor; any tendency in side-by-sides to shoot in the opposite direction to their cast as a result of recoil forces at the shoulder may be compensated for by flexure in the grip. I tend not to use much cast in over-and-unders for this reason.

shooter than a conventional design. On some ported guns, for example those made by Beretta and Browning this extra blast is barely noticeable, on others, older Winchesters for example, it can be quite severe. Porting can also lead to ribs become heated more quickly than they might, which can cause the irritating problem of heat 'shimmer'. Another small disadvantage of porting is that it increases cleaning time.

**Recoil reducers** are a device more commonly seen in the United States than in Britain (although Alan Rhone is offering to supply and fit them in the UK). There are a number of different makes on the market working on different principles. Some are filled with mercury, the best known is the 'Edwards Recoil Reducer,' a cylindrical device made in various sizes, typically about five inches long and one inch wide. The stock must be drilled to accommodate an Edwards type reducer. I have not examined one internally, but presume it works on an inertial system with a piston and some sort of damping. When the gun is fired, this mechanism absorbs recoil energy. How well the Edwards and similar devices work is open to some argument; their extra weight, however, must have some recoil reduction effect although it will also change the gun's balance.

### Telescopic Stocks
Also on the American market are various devices which turn the gun stock itself into a telescopic shock-absorber. Some work on a hydraulic principle, others are pneumatic for lighter weight. These devices, made by companies like Hydro-Coil, Allison and Carey and Soft Touch and rarely seen in Great Britain, are complicated and difficult and expensive to fit. They can be very effective, however, reducing felt recoil and muzzle flip dramatically. I have shot several and they all seem to work as advertised. Altough one might expect otherwise, the movement of the mechanism on these devices on the first shot has no practical affect on the second.

### Cheek Pads
The nearest the British have yet come to any of these devices is the padded cheekpiece which was a popular accessory in the eighteenth century, but which managed to survive into the twentieth in the form of a rubber comb insert.

### Recoil Pads
Recoil pads can offer a convenient means to add length to a gun stock, as well as reducing felt recoil. Many different patterns are available. The classic pad par excellence was made by the firm of Silvers. A very similar pad is made today by Griffen & Howe. These solid pads are designed to be fitted to the gun, ground to the right contour, and then 'burnt off' to achieve a smooth finish. They are elegant but expensive and quite heavy, and are not as effective at absorbing recoil as some of the modern pads. I still like them because they are so easy to grind to shape.

All sorts of recoil pads are available now: ventilated trap types in which there is a marked hollow in the middle of the butt and a serrated rear surface for better grip; interchangeable pads which allow alterations for length; the

German type of pad which has a hard, smooth heel made of hard plastic and which is designed not to catch at the heel in mounting; finally, one ought to mention the 'high-tech' type of pad made of new materials (like 'Sorbothane') with vastly improved recoil absorption properties. Gunfitters should be careful that when pads are fitted to customer's guns they specify clearly how they should be finished at the butt sole. In particular, the subtle shaping which is important to some shooters – notably the slight bump just below the heel – is sometimes lost. I do not like the pads with a hard plastic insert at the heel very much even though it is often suggested that they prevent snagging. They reduce effective contact with the shoulder in the vital top two inches of the butt sole, the area which forms the pivot about which the gun rotates in recoil.

We might also note the existence of leather covered recoil pads, the obvious advantages of which are their non-sticky surface and pleasing appearance. Some are not fully covered in the English fashion, but merely have a piece of leather glued to their rear; this is a simple and effective way to prevent a rubber pad sticking, and it does not wear off as varnish does. All pads (and indeed butts) intended for sporting clays and skeet, where quick mounting is important, should have a well rounded heel so as not to catch clothing.

Pad selection will depend not only on the client's chosen shotgun sport, but on his or her mounting style. The experienced American stockmaker, Reinhart Fajen, notes:

> Location of the butt plate, or pad, is very important. Generally, recoil should be taken on the muscles in the shoulder and chest area. The butt plate should be placed so that the 2 or 3 inches in the center or soft part of the recoil pad, fits solidly and squarely against this area. This avoids the hard top or bottom of the pad from punishing the shooter and helps put the butt plate consistently in the correct place. If contact of the butt is made on the shoulder, away from the chest, a curved trap-type pad is recommended ... If contact is made closer on the chest, a flat Skeet-type pad may be called for ...

Fitting recoil pads is an art in itself. Modern gunmakers seem to pay insufficient attention to the strap and butt soles/recoil pads. Yet a gun can be transformed by correct fitting of these subtle variations.

## Weight

In putting effort into fitting a gun to an individual we are trying to produce a gun which handles well for that individual. Handling involves balance and weight as well as physical dimensions.

A great deal of opinion has been presented as fact on the subject of gun weight and balance. I shall endeavour not to make the same mistake. How much should a gun weigh? Whatever suits the user. Forget the old idea of multiplying the shot charge weight by a constant. The typical weight for a post–1918 English side-by-side 12 bore was about 6¹/₂ lb. Wildfowling guns have traditionally been a little heavier. Today, most over-and-under competition guns fall between 7¹/₂ and 8¹/₂ lb. In the United States some skeet and trap shooters prefer even heavier guns. The light gun is less effort to carry and swings easily, at least initially (both of which may be important in game shooting). The heavy gun is smooth to shoot, recoils less, and follows through more easily. One can point to some great sporting shots who use relatively light guns (John Bidwell), others who use fairly heavy guns (Barry Simpson and George Digweed). It boils down to individual preference, but it is interesting to note that some of the great feats of shotgun marksmanship in the late nineteenth century were accomplished with guns weighing ten pounds or more.

## Balance

Some experts will tell you that a shotgun should balance on its hinge pin, but many shooters will find their swing is smoother if the gun balances just forward of the hinge pin. Skeet shooters, in particular, seem to like guns which are quite muzzle-heavy. Some experts also suggest that a well-balanced gun is one in which the weight is 'between the hands'; they suggest that this as an inherent advantage of the sidelock design: its heavier mechanism and sideplates put extra weight between the hands. This may be so, but extraordinary feats of shooting have been accomplished by pump and semi-automatic shotguns which, to my mind at least, balance like old bits of drain pipe.

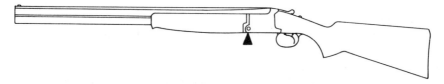

I prefer a gun to balance on the hinge pin or very slightly forward of it.

Bearing all the above in mind, I might venture the comment that the balance requirements of a game gun are probably different to those of a clay gun. A game gun, especially one to be used at targets like grouse early in the season, wants to be fairly lively. It should therefore not weigh too much, and may well benefit from a balance which is on the pin (though, interestingly, Purdeys usually balance just forward of the pin). A gun intended for English Sporting or English or NSSA skeet on the other hand (where steadiness is essential for winning scores), wants to be both heavier and more neutral in its balance characteristics. Only experience can dictate what is right for a particular individual; my preference in 28 in. and 30 in. guns is a balance on the hinge pin, a little forward of its centre on 32 in. guns.

*How to change balance:* Weight can be introduced into the stock by means of lead glued in position, or by using heavy lead shot in putty. Weight may be taken from a stock by drilling or otherwise hollowing it or removing wood from the onside of the stock. Weight can be added to barrels by using glaziers' lead strip (the type used for fake leaded windows) or purpose-made barrel weight attached at the muzzle or in the forend. Weight can be taken from the barrels by overboring them, and, at least on over-and-unders, by removing, partially removing, or lightening the joining ribs.

## Do-It-Yourself Gunfitting

The shooter who wants his gun fitted must make a choice: he or she may visit a professional instructor/fitter with a pattern plate and a store of knowledge or they may attempt the job themselves. There is something to be said for either course of action. If one does not have much interest in the subject of gunfit and is lucky enough to possess an expensive gun from a famous maker, then it makes sense to consult a professional with an established reputation. However, there are some important advantages to the do-it-yourself route. First, it is cheap (some people simply cannot afford the cost of a fitting – usually about double that of an ordinary lesson). Second – and it applies particularly to the serious competitor – one can find out a great deal about one's shooting from the do-it-yourself approach.

Any amateur gunfitter would be well advised to team up with a friend who is an experienced shot. Both should keep in mind the golden rules of gun fitting as mentioned in the Introduction: be methodical; be cautious; and be patient.

## Alterations to Gun Stocks

So far, we have not talked much about the actual business of physically altering gun stocks. Apart from actually shaving wood off the comb or inletting a piece into the gun stock, there are three principle methods by which the cast and drop dimensions of a gun stock may be altered.

The first, which has much to recommend it on competition guns because it is unlikely ever to be affected by atmospheric conditions, is to make adjustments 'at the head', that part of the gunstock which meets the back of the action. Minute amounts of wood removed at the head by a skilled stocker will allow the stock to be brought up or down, or pushed to one side or the other. This method of adjusting cast and drop has the further advantage of not effecting stock finish.

Another excellent method for making adjustments to drop and cast is by the application of heat from infra-red lamps at the grip area while the gunstock is subjected to pressure in a jig. When this system is used, the stocker must always over-adjust the stock which when it cools down will tend to move back towards the original dimensions.

The traditional method for making adjustments to cast and drop, and probably the worst in my opinion, is the application of hot oil or steam to the gun stock while it is placed in a jig. The principle is the same as for the infra-red method, but the hot-oil method has the distinct disadvantage of staining the gun stock at the grip (although the stain will be almost undetectable when the work is carried out by a craftsman). All methods of altering stock dimensions by the application of heat involve a small risk of breakage. Fitters should also be aware that because of the imprecision of some methods guns are likely to be returned to them which have not been altered as requested. The only answer is to develop a relationship with a stocker whose work one trusts.

### NOTES

1   I have found very small changes in rib height and pitch can be an important part of the fine tuning process of serious competition guns. As already noted, I think this is a neglected area. I would also note that I think the rib pitch on many mass-produced over-and-unders is wrong. I think most would benefit from more depth of rib at the muzzles. This pitch could then be combined with a higher stock/comb, reducing recoil and increasing target visibility.

# FINAL CONCLUSIONS

There is a large amount of information packed in to this book; no-one unfamiliar with the subject is going to take it in at a single reading, or indeed just by reading. There is simply no substitute for experience. I want to finish by making two points. First, I note that many gunfit problems are actually problems of poor design. Too many guns are being produced today which are not suited to any user. In particular, combs are often unnecessarily inclined and thick in the wrong place (both features which increase recoil), grips are often poorly shaped and difficult to hold in recoil, and, in the case of over-and-unders especially, insufficient attention has been paid to barrel and rib regulation. I would like to see more over-and-unders set up so that one could see more rib (and hence more target) without the guns being prone to high shooting. This would entail making their ribs deeper at the muzzles.

My second and final point is simple but important. The primary aim when gun fitting should be to produce a gun which flows with hands and eye – a gun which is as unnoticeable to the shooter as possible. The well-fitted gun promotes consistency and economy of movement in shooting, and turns the act of shooting into a single, graceful, flowing motion. Anything which impedes that flow or which disrupts the relationship between eye and target is an indication of poor fit.

# SELECT BIBLIOGRAPHY

Akehurst, Richard, *Game Guns and Rifles*, The Sportsman's Press, London, 1992 (new edition).

Andersson, Stellan and Akerman, Jan, *The Practical Gun*, Macdonald Queen Anne Press, London, 1986.

Arthur, Robert, *The Shotgun Stock*, A.S. Barnes & Co., Inc., Cranbury, New Jersey, 1971.

Askins, Charles, *The American Shotgun*, Wolfe Publishing Co., Prescott, Arizona, 1987 (facsimile edition).

Bentley, Paul, *Clay Target Shooting*, Adam and Charles Black, London, 1981.

Bentley, Paul, *Competitive Clay Target Shooting*, Adam and Charles Black, London, 1991.

Bidwell, John with Scott, Robin, *Move, Mount, Shoot*, The Crowood Press, Marlborough, 1990.

Blatt, Art, *The Gun Digest Book of Trap & Skeet Shooting*, DBI Books Inc., Northfield, Illinois, 1984.

Bogardus, Adam H., *Field, Cover and Trap Shooting*, A.H. Bogardus, New York, 1878.

Bowlen, Bruce, *The Orvis Wing-Shooting Handbook*, Nick Lyons Books, New York, 1985.

Brindle, John, *Shotgun Shooting, Techniques and Technology*, Nimrod Book Services, Liss, Hampshire, 1985.

Brister, Bob, *Shotgunning: The Art and the Science*, Winchester Press, Tulsa, Oklahoma, 1976.

Burrard, Bt, DSO, Major Sir Gerald, *The Modern Shotgun*, Vol. III, 'The Gun and the Cartridge', The Field Library, Ashford Press Publishing, Southampton, 1985 (facsimile edition).

Chevenix Trench, Charles, *History of Marksmanship*, Longman, London, 1972.

Churchill, Robert, *Game Shooting*, Michael Joseph, London, 1963.

Cradock, Chris, *A Manual of Clayshooting*, B.T. Batsford, London, 1988.

Davies, Ken, *The Better Shot*, Quiller Press, London, 1992.

*Encyclopaedia of Firearms*, edited by Harold L. Peterson, The Connoisseur, George Rainbird Ltd, London, 1964.

Greener, W.W., *The Gun and its Development*, Arms and Armour Press Ltd.,

London, 1986 (facsimile edition).

Hartman, Barney, *Hartman on Skeet*, McLelland and Stewart Ltd, Toronto, 1973.

Hastings, Macdonald, *The Shotgun*, David and Charles, London 1981.

Hawker, Lt-Col P., *Instructions to Young Sportsmen*, Herbert Jenkins, London, 1922 (first edition 1833).

Hearn, Arthur, *Shooting and Gunfitting*, Herbert Jenkins, London.

Hinman, Bob, *The Golden Age of Shotgunning*, Wolfe Publishing Co., Prescott, Arizona, 1982.

Keith, Elmer, *Shotguns by Keith*, Wolfe Publishing Co., Prescott, Arizona, 1988 (facsimile edition).

Lancaster, Charles, *The Art of Shooting*, Ashford Press Publishing, Southampton, 1985 (facsimile edition).

Martin, Dr Wayne, *An Insight to Sports: Featuring Trapshooting and Golf*, Sportsvision Inc., Seattle, 1984.

Ohye, Kaye, *You and the Target*, Scattergun Press, Austin, Texas, 1987.

Blair, Claude (ed), Pollard's History of Firearms, Country Life Books.

O'Connor, Jack, *Complete Book of Shooting*, Outdoor Life, Harper & Row, New York, 1965.

Purdey, T.D.S. & Purdey, Capt. J.A., *The Shot Gun*, Vol. 20, The Sportsman's Library, Adam and Charles Black, London, 1947.

Reynolds, Mike, with Barnes, Mike, *Shooting Made Easy*, The Crowood Press, Marlborough, 1986.

Smith, A.J., *Sporting Clays*, Argus Books, Hemel Hempstead, 1989.

Smith, A.M., *Sporting Clays Master Class*, Argus Books, Hemel Hempstead, 1991.

Stanbury, Percy and Carlisle, G.L., *Clay Pigeon Marksmanship*, Barrie & Jenkins, London, 1982.

Stanbury, Percy and Carlisle, G.L., *Shotgun Marksmanship*, Herbert Jenkins, London, 1965.

Teasdale-Buckell, G.T., *The Complete Shot*, Methuen & Co., London, 1907.

Teasdale-Buckell, G.T., *Experts on Guns and Shooting*, The Field Library, Ashford Press Publishing, Southampton, 1986 (facsimile edition).

Thomas, Gough, *Shooting Facts and Fancies*, Adam and Charles Black, London, 1978.

Thomas, Gough, *Gun Book*, Adams and Charles Black, London, 1983.

Thomas, Gough, *Shotguns & Cartridges for Game and Clays*, Adam and Charles Black, London, 1975.

Walsh, J.H., *The Modern Sportsman's Gun and Rifle*, Horace Cox, The Field Office, London, 1882.

Zutz, Don, *Shotgunning: Trends in Transition*, Wolfe Publishing Company, Prescott, Arizona, 1989.

# INDEX